POLICY IN URBAN PLANNING

POLICY IN URBAN PLANNING

Structure plans, programmes and local plans

WILLIAM SOLESBURY

PERGAMON PRESS

Oxford · New York · Toronto · Sydney

Pergamon Press Ltd., Headington Hill Hall, Oxford
Pergamon Press Inc., Maxwell House, Fairview Park, Elmsford,
New York 10523
Pergamon of Canada Ltd., 207 Queen's Quay West, Toronto 1
Pergamon Press (Aust.) Pty. Ltd., 19a Boundary Street,
Rushcutters Bay, N.S.W. 2011, Australia

First edition 1974

Library of Congress Cataloging in Publication Data

Solesbury, William.
Policy in urban planning.

(Urban and regional planning series, v. 8)
Bibliography: p.
1. Cities and towns—Planning—1945
I. Title. II. Series.
HT166.S63 1974   309.2'62   74–7004
ISBN 0–08–017758–1

**Urban and Regional Planning Series
Volume 8**

Printed in Great Britain by A. Wheaton & Co., Exeter.

To Felicity, Tara and Eliza

Contents

Introduction

PLANS and the making of plans have exercised a continuing fascination in planning. Indeed the purpose and main activity of planners is conventionally regarded by professionals, politicians and the public as the making of plans of various kinds: regional plans, transportation plans, redevelopment plans and others. While being concerned with plans and the making of plans, this book seeks to relegate them in importance. Plans cannot exist usefully for themselves. Their role is as the policy element in administrative systems focused on the control of change. It is executive decisions which are the instruments of that control, not the statements of policy, but the policies or plans are essential prerequisites for an effective use of those instruments.

The basic intention in this book is to present a view of the nature of policy in urban planning and to assess the potential of the kinds of policy statement which are currently available for the expression of such policy. Thus Part One is concerned with the kinds and processes of change which urban planning administratively seeks to control. In particular Chapter 1 defines the processes generating societal changes and identifies those classes of change with which planning concerns itself. Chapter 2 then looks at the agents of local environmental change—the consumers, operators, developers, local and central government—and the systems of incentives which motivate their actions. Chapter 3 elaborates on the role of the local authority through a simple model of the operation of their control over environmental change: in this, situations arise in the community, issues are recognised as calling for responses from the authority, their decision on a choice of action is taken and followed by its execution to effect a consequent change in the original situation. Policy exists to guide such executive decisions towards greater equity and effectiveness.

Part Two considers the expression of policy. Chapter 4 discusses the basic forms which policy can take and the languages in which it can be expressed to enhance its relevance to executive decision making and its general comprehensibility. Chapter 5 traces the implications for policy statements of some

1

characteristics of the kinds of issues with which urban planning deals: these implications are the necessity of both areal and topical expressions of policy, of both strategic and tactical policy and the choice between static and dynamic treatments of time. Chapter 6 presents an account of the variety of policy statements in urban planning, notably development plans together with the common forms of informal policy statement like, for example, village plans and transportation study reports; it also discusses ways in which the overall policy framework for urban planning is changing. Within this framework Chapters 7, 8 and 9 deal with the form and content of structure plans, programmes and local plans respectively.

Part Three is concerned with the making of policy and Chapter 10 draws together the considerations affecting the evaluative, analytical and consultative tasks of policy making and review which arise from the nature and expression of policy itself. Thus the argument of the book runs from the nature of environmental change to the executive decisions of local authorities seeking to control that change, to the necessity of policy to guide such executive decisions, to the nature of that policy and the ways in which it can be expressed, to the kinds of plan or policy statement defined by statute or custom available for its expression, and finally to the process of making and reviewing such policy statements. Underlying this argument are three propositions: these concern the role of plans or policy in urban planning, the characteristics of urban planning as a field of public administration and the dual technical and political nature of planning policy.

PLAN MAKING AND PLANNING

The view that planning and implementation are two distinct processes is here consciously rejected. According to this view planning is concerned with formulating plans, implementation is concerned with carrying them out.[1] The implication is that without the plan the environment would not change. This may be true of the plan for a building or a machine which is usually to be construed as a specification for its construction, since the making of the plan and the changes which realise the plan are linked by a clear chain of control, usually involving the same deciders: the plan is commissioned by those who undertake the action.

But this is not true of urban planning. The broader changes in the environments of town and countryside with which planning is concerned are occur-

ring all the time, with or without a plan. And the public authorities charged
with responsibilities relating to the environment will be acting all the time,
undertaking, regulating or inducing change, again with or without a plan:
neither their statutory responsibilities, nor the communities to whom they
are accountable, nor the political or professional motivations of those within
the authorities will for long tolerate inaction in the face of environmental
change. But equally they will not tolerate capricious or ineffective action. So
that while the commitment to executive decision and action in general may
not be dependent on the prior existence of a plan, the precise choice of
decision on a particular issue can be more effective, less capricious if it is
guided by a plan or policy for dealing with that class of issue. In this way the
plan is not the mainspring to executive decisions and actions but it is a guide
to the choice of decision and action. In this context the term "plan" with its
suggestion of finality of intent and direct, consequential action is something
of a misnomer; "policy" provides a better expression of the nature of that
kind of statement in urban planning.

Planning must not then be equated with plan making, for this is only part
of it. Public authorities with urban planning responsibilities make decisions
other than the policy decisions in plans, their staffs engage in activities other
than the making and reviewing of plans. At any point in time most of their
effort is expended inevitably and rightly on the executive decisions which
really influence the changes in the environment. The ways in which policy is
expressed must reflect the ways in which these executive decisions are to be
taken, so that the relevance of policy to the situations and issues calling for
responses is apparent. In these circumstances the form in which policy is
expressed, as various kinds of norm or standard against which to measure
prospective changes, and the language in which it is expressed, whether
verbal, mathematical or iconic, are important: all these are discussed further
in Chapters 4 and 5.

Plan or policy making is not the sole, or even the prime activity in urban
planning, nor is it unique to it. If the focus of planning is shifted from plans
to executive decisions and it is recognised that the significance of plans is as
policy to guide execution, then it is clear that policy is necessary and desirable
in any field of public administration, or indeed private management, when
some control needs to be exercised over diverse agents of change in order to
attain the desired ends of the controlling interest. The purpose and nature of
urban planning cannot therefore be defined in methodological terms since it

shares much of its policy making methodology with other fields of policy. Indeed it is this recognition of the need for policy outside the field of planning that has produced the explosion of ideas on decision making that has so noticeably fertilised urban planning itself in the last decade[2]—ideas on analysis, on modelling, on evaluation and so on which are considered further in Chapter 10. Urban planning must be defined in substantive, rather than methodological, terms as a field of public administration concerned with particular classes of change in the community while sharing in the characteristics of public administration in general.

PLANNING AS PUBLIC ADMINISTRATION

In the workings of society a distinction is recognised between those changes which are secured by acts of private entrepreneurship and those secured by acts of public administration. The distinction is between those situations in which an individual chooses for himself and those in which one, albeit a collective one, chooses for many. The first can be called market choice, not because a cash transaction is necessarily involved but because the chooser decides principally on the basis of the utility to himself alone. The second can be called political choice. The last century and a half have been characterised by a continued expansion in the scope of political choice.[3] Market choice mediates transactions which are reciprocal; but the transactions which can be regarded as simply reciprocal have diminished as the public interest has become more pervasive. So that government has created public agencies to supplant markets for the provision of certain kinds of goods and services or has established regulatory powers to secure the public interest in the operation of markets. In this period planning, like education or social welfare, has emerged as a concern of government and as a field of public administration as part of this process of ever extending public interest.[4]

Five classes of condition provide rationales for the exercise of political choice.[5]

(i) There are the so-called public goods which, if supplied to one are supplied to all and which cost no more to supply each additional person. Consequently it is impossible or difficult to price their supply to exclude non-paying consumers, and so these goods and services tend to be supplied by public agencies and financed through general taxation. Broadcasting, roads, national defence, clean air are examples.

(ii) There are other goods and services which, apart from their utility to the consumer, create as side effects or externalities social benefits or disbenefits for others not directly consuming them. Again there is a social value which it is difficult to reflect in a market price. The treatment of contagious diseases is an example of the creation of social benefits, reducing as it does the risk to others as well as curing the of invalid. Pollution in its various forms exemplifies the creation of social disbenefits, for the disposal on land or in the water or the air the wastes generated by particular activities diminishes the utility of land, water or air for others who wish to use them. Public agencies must either supply themselves or regulate in some way the supply of goods and services with important externalities, setting the level of the supply as an act of political choice having regard to the social benefits and disbenefits created.

(iii) There are also certain high-cost, high-risk goods and services which are too expensive or uncertain as investments for private entrepreneurs and which justify the creation of natural monopolies to provide them. Governments with their access to vast financial resources, their freedom from the dangers of insolvency and their power to restrict competitive activities can undertake investments that are out of the question for private capital. The provision of public utilities like gas, electricity, sewerage and telecommunications as well as advanced technologies like aerospace and computers are examples.

(iv) There is also a need for public regulation of complex interactions where a public agency acting as broker, referee or clearing house can secure a better outcome for all than acts of market choice alone. This can be achieved through the exchange of information to avoid the hazards of mutual ignorance: the traffic signal is a simple example. It might equally involve the exchange of assets which can produce a greater overall benefit: land assembly, comprehensive development and redevelopment are examples.

(v) There is finally what might be termed paternalistic regulation to prevent self-injurious actions or encourage self-enhancing actions by individuals, even though no benefits or disbenefits will accrue to others. The rationale for paternalism is that government has greater wisdom about what is harmful or helpful to individuals than they themselves do. Thus there is compulsory school attendance, support for arts and recreation and selective censorship. A variation on this rationale exists where paternalistic regulation is intended to conserve benefits for future generations. Consumers are typically inclined to sacrifice future for present pleasures so that, for example, without public intervention there would be a tendency for rapid exhaustion of raw materials and deterioration of the environment. Conservation then becomes a responsibility of public administration.

Any particular field of public administration needs justification in terms of one or more of these rationales. Their relevance to the processes of environmental change must be apparent. Four of them in particular have been important in the development of urban planning as a proper field for public administration—the public goods, social benefit, complex interactions and conservation rationales. Many urban services have come to be accepted as pure public goods, notably roads and open spaces, and orderly urban development has long presupposed public provision of these basic services. At the same time public responsibility has come to be accepted for the quality of air and water courses. Equally it has long been clear that urban activities and development produce side effects which may be beneficial or harmful; in a sense the environment is largely the incidental creation of changes primarily directed towards far narrower ends. Thus the regulation of such changes in order to diminish social disbenefits and enhance social benefits has been a central concern of planning. Then, because land ownerships are so fragmented and the processes of environmental change involve so many agents, planning has accepted the task of easing the processes of change through procedures for mediating and allocating among competing demands. Finally, because land is a finite resource and environmental changes are largely irreversible by future generations, regulation of these changes has become accepted as necessary to safeguard future as well as present public interests.

Resting on these rationales there has developed a distinct field of public administration concerned with bringing the public interest to bear on the complex and continuing processes by which the environment of town and countryside changes over time. This is the field of planning which one might define as that field of public administration concerned with the control of systemic change in the physical environment.[6] Chapter 2 discusses further the kinds of action which local authorities and central government pursue as part of this control. Planning's initial concern with the forms of development by which land is adapted for different or more intensive use has been extended successively to embrace concern with changes in the nature of the uses or activities themselves, with their locational relationships and, in particular, the modification of those relationships through changes in transport systems, as well as with the quality of the external environment which developments, activities and uses create. And like all fields of public administration, urban planning has accumulated minor concerns and responsibilities which only fit untidily within it and at its edges it shades fuzzily into other fields. Its limits have become essentially matters of administrative custom and convenience. Chapter 5 discusses this fact in relation to both topics and areas for policy. But at urban planning's core is a closely related set of issues, institutions, powers, professions and ideologies with sufficient coherence to be regarded as a distinct field of public action.

PLANNING AND POLITICS

If planning is regarded as a field of public administration then it must be closely involved with politics. Attempts are sometimes made to deny the political nature of planning, to regard the issues with which planning is concerned as amenable to technical solutions and to believe that such solutions would command widespread support because they are based upon a broad consensus about objectives and promulgated by professionals who command respect for their skills and knowledge. According to this view the frequent intrusion of politics to modify, support or suppress technically excellent decisions inevitably leads to distortion of these decisions. But this idea that planning could be insulated from political disputation was never very realistic.[7]

For one thing it encouraged a greater reliance upon technical expertise than the professionals in planning could possibly deliver. The concepts and techniques which planning adopted as it emerged as a separate field were essentially those of engineering.[8] In designing a bridge the objective is known and once the brief regarding siting, capacity, hydrological conditions and cost limits is ready, the designer is in almost complete charge of the processes by which the project will be realised and he has at its command a mass of knowledge expressed in technical rules of proven validity concerning structural stability, vehicle-lane capacities, durability of materials and so on. But a decision to attract new industrial firms to a hitherto predominantly dormitory town is a very different kind of decision. Here the objectives may be multiple and not universally agreed, the means may be partly in the hands of others who must be persuaded or compelled to act, techniques may be incapable of providing very certain predictions of the consequences of different actions. In short, such a decision is likely to stir up political controversy when compared to the design of a bridge.

Political controversy arises out of conflicts.[9] The existence of conflict in society arises from the inequalities in society: inequalities of incomes and possessions, inequalities of knowledge and experience, inequalities of access to political power, inequalities in locational situations—the interests of different areas and the interests of larger areas against those of their component parts—and inequalities of outlook and imagination. The existence of these differences means that society is pluralist—composed of individuals and groups with differing goals, beliefs and attitudes, all of which merit respect. That being so, it must be evident that decisions in planning, no less than in any other field of public administration, affect those interests differentially—benefiting some and disbenefiting others. Chapter 3 discusses the influence of politics on the recognition of issues for executive decisions and Chapter 10 discusses the role of politics in policy making and review.

The two examples—the bridge design as a technical decision and the industrial development programme as a political decision—represent extreme cases. In practice most choices in urban planning embrace both technics and politics in various degrees. The currency of technics is facts, the currency of politics is values. Facts are objectively verifiable statements about the nature of the real world. Values are statements of preference regarding the nature of the real world. Values, unlike facts, cannot be proved correct or incorrect—they can only be approved as right or condemned as wrong.[10] Decisions in planning, being partly technical and partly political, must be based therefore on both factual and value judgements. Furthermore, there is a close relationship between these two elements for, on the one hand, facts can only be regarded as relevant to a decision in relation to some judgement of value and, on the other hand, judgements of value are operative only in relation to some set of available facts.[11] This interaction between what is known as a fact and what is held as a value is a recurring theme in planning decisions and underlies the balance between technics and politics which is at the heart of urban planning.

Where choices are recognised as raising issues of technics and of politics, then the technical considerations are conventionally regarded as the preserve of the professional in public administration whereas political considerations are for the politician to resolve. But the close interplay between facts and values precludes such a neat division of responsibilities. The exercise of the professional's technical skills cannot be entirely value-free. Nor can the politician's value judgement be made without some recognition of the limitations of factual knowledge within which he is operating. The proper marriage of technics and politics in planning is always threatened by opposing tendencies: to professionalise decision making by overstressing technics without recognition of its implicit value judgements or to politicise decision making by overreliance on political value judgement insufficiently informed by factual knowledge. This is discussed further in Chapter 10.

These three propositions—that plans derive their validity from executive decisions rather than vice versa, that urban planning must be seen in an administrative context and that the role of politics must be explicitly recognised—underlie much of what follows. This is not therefore a technical or an administrative or a political view of policy in urban planning but a synthesis of all three aspects. To illustrate this point it can be noted that in the course of the following chapters a great diversity of considerations are brought to bear on the use, expression and making of policy, including the effect of ward representation on councillors' perceptions of issues, the distinctions between strategic and tactical policy, the varying replacement rates for buildings of different types, the comparative expressiveness of verbal and mathematical languages, the choice between optimising and satisficing in reaching decisions and the relative responsibilities of counties and districts after local government reorganisation. Hopefully the attempt at synthesis creates a pattern which is both recognisable and illuminating.

ACKNOWLEDGEMENTS

I would like to thank innumerable colleagues whose ideas on policy and policy making in urban planning have mingled so with mine that some of them might reasonably consider themselves co-authors of parts of the book; particular thanks go to Susan Barrett and Edward Craven who commented on the book in draft. Other thanks go to my wife Felicity and friends Diane and Alan Ritch who responded to an emergency and co-operated in typing the manuscript. Finally, it must be added that the views in the book, particularly the views on the statutory development plan system, are of course my own.

Berkeley, California   WILLIAM SOLESBURY

PART ONE

The Need for Policy

CHAPTER 1

Activities, Resources and Change

ALL public administration is concerned with human activities, with what the community, individually and collectively, wants to do with its money, time, skills and energy. More specifically public administration is concerned with changes in human activities. It exists to control certain classes of change in human activities which it is felt, by common agreement, should not be left to be determined by market choice alone. This is clearly as true of education, social welfare, the management of the economy, the administration of justice as it is of that field of public administration called planning. In each of these fields rationales exist to justify interventions by public authorities in the flows of money, goods, services, information and satisfactions which make up human activities.*

Activities make demands on resources. It is the continual allocation of resources to activities which provides the motive power of change. The classical resource trinity is of land resources, capital resources and human resources.[1] Land resources include not just the land and its topography, but its locational characteristics, the natural resources of minerals and vegetation and the resources of air and water, all with aesthetic as well as economic values. Capital resources are the accumulations of wealth in the community which can be mobilised to finance the creation of capital assets of plant and machinery, vehicles and buildings. Human resources are the most varied of all, comprising the population with its diversity of perceptions, values, experiences, skills and abilities. This variety of resources becomes committed in varying degrees to the pursuit of human activities. Land, air and water become utilised, human resources become engaged in production or consumption, capital is turned into structures and equipment. And by such processes changes in human activity are generated and sustained.

* See Introduction.

13

But, despite this close connection between activities and resource utilisation, probably the bulk of the changes in activities in the community make no additional claims on human, land or capital resources. These are changes in the behaviour patterns of individuals, households, institutions and firms by which they adjust to changes in external circumstances or shifts in their own values: for example, changes in the choice of travel routes, changes in hours of working and sleeping, changes in routine office procedures or retailing practices can occur without making any substantial demand on capital, without producing any significant change in land use and without having any great impact on people's lives. Minor changes of this kind go on

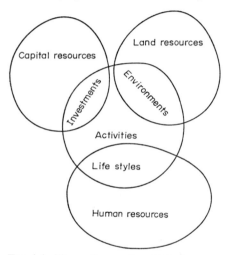

Fig. 1.1. Three classes of societal change.

all the time, almost unnoticed. Numerically they represent the majority of changes but in terms of their impact on the totality of human activity and its claims on resources they are of much lesser importance. Consequently, by both custom and law, public administration seeks no powers of control over this mass of minor changes. Rather it tends to be concerned with the major changes in activities. And it is these changes which generally relate most crucially to resource use.

These relationships between resources and activities define three classes of change illustrated in Fig. 1.1. The relationship between human resources and activities creates the differing combinations of opportunities which are available to different groups in the community, commonly called differences in life style. The relationship between capital and activities creates the pattern and process of investment by which capital is allocated to different activities. The relationship between land and activities leads to changes in land use and development which together mould the physical environment. Of these the latter is clearly of greatest significance for urban planning, but the other two have some importance and relevance.

LIFE STYLES

Differing life styles are manifested in two ways in the community: tangibly in terms of patterns of expenditure of money and time, abstractly in terms of the systems of personal beliefs and attitudes which underlie such behaviours. Thus groups in the community with particular attitudes and backgrounds tend to work in particular jobs, have particular housing conditions and particular consumption patterns, get educated in particular ways and share particular leisure pursuits. That they do so is largely a product of the opportunities available to them, including their state of information about and their evaluation of those activities, as well as the means of access to them and their funds of time or money for availing themselves of the opportunities. These complex meshes of interrelationship between people and activities represent different life styles.[2]

Particularly important in influencing life style is occupation. For most people work is the major or only source of income and hence the chief influence on the pattern of their demand for goods and services. But more than that, the position taken by households in the social structure is largely based on the occupation of the chief earner in the household. And additionally occupations typically develop a culture which not only determines what is appropriate at work but also influences beliefs and behaviour outside work. By these processes occupation and social status become associated with distinctive styles of life.

Statistical data on the prevalence of different life styles in the community is hard to assemble.[3] Statistics of income and expenditure are relatively poorly developed, particularly below the national, fairly aggregate level.[4] The closest proxy for life styles available in standard data sources are the socio-economic groups of the national census which are intended to classify together people whose social, cultural and recreational standards and behaviour are similar.[5] In a sense this is a measure of life-style differences. But in the absence of direct information on these matters in the census, people are allocated to socio-economic groups according to the employment status and occupation of household heads. One fairly detailed published regional analysis identifies three groups which can be differentiated in occupational terms: what is called the senior salariat, the middle mass and the semi-skilled and unskilled.[6] Table 1.1 shows the percentage composition of the national work force in these terms in 1961.

TABLE 1.1. SOCIO-ECONOMIC GROUPS
IN THE U.K. 1961

Senior salariat	16%
Middle mass	44%
Semi-skilled	25% ⎫ 40%
Unskilled	15% ⎭

Source: derived from South-east Joint Planning Team (1971), *Strategic Plan for the South East,* Studies Vol. No. 2, H.M.S.O., London, chap. 2, based in turn upon Ministry of Labour (1967), *Manpower Studies* No. 6: *Occupational Changes* 1957–61, H.M.S.O., London.

To these it adds two groups which cannot be categorised in occupational terms: the wealthy élite and the least privileged groups, other than the unskilled and semi-skilled, such as the old, disabled and deviants.

In the south-east region the life styles of these five groups are categorised in these terms:

(i) the élite—a small minority group, its income largely derived from inherited capital, very mobile, with houses, or at least *pied-à-terre* in central London;

(ii) the senior salariat—a fast-growing group, its income derived from highly paid professional and managerial work requiring high qualifications, long hours of work, with limited leisure opportunities except for holidays, residing either rurally with long distance commuting or centrally;

(iii) the middle mass—a predominant group, with medium incomes derived from technical, clerical and skilled manual work of strictly limited and diminishing hours, displaying increasing emphasis on the home and leisure pursuits and growing concern with education, residing predominantly in owner-occupied and selected local authority suburban housing areas; but within this general life style there is much variety of consumption despite the similarity of income;

(iv) the semi-skilled and unskilled—a large slowly diminishing group, with relatively low incomes from poorly paid, chiefly manual work, residing frequently in inadequate rented housing in older housing areas, with expenditure biased heavily towards the essentials of rent and food;

(v) the least privileged—a small minority group with low incomes deriving principally from sources other than employment but otherwise similar in residence and expenditure to the semi-skilled and unskilled.

Changes in life style occur continuously as patterns of activity change. Since jobs, housing and education seem important influences on life styles it is changes in these activities which have particularly significant effects. In particular, employment is the mainspring of much social and geographic mobility which is itself an important process by which changes in life style occur. But education is also important, especially in the longer term, both in influencing people's position in the job market and in influencing the tastes which determine their expenditure of time and money. But if changing job and educational opportunities are important influences upon changing life styles, then the location and kind of housing in which people live is a major constraint on their ability or propensity to take advantage of these changing opportunities.

And yet life style is the outcome of something more than the particular opportunities available to members of the community and the means they have of availing themselves of them. Their aspirations are also important, and may run counter to the more tangible influences. So that despite the structural change in job markets, educational systems or housing markets there can be remarkable persistence of beliefs and attitudes, for example, when families move from the inner areas of cities to their suburbs.[7] Life style evolves then in response to these two pressures: relatively rapid changes in activity systems and slower changes in underlying beliefs and attitudes.

INVESTMENTS

Human activities embrace activities of both production and consumption. Between consumers and producers and between producers themselves there are constant flows of goods and money. The goods comprise both consumer goods and services and capital goods; money comprises flows of wages, rents, dividends, taxes and expenditure. The expenditure of consumers provides demand for consumer goods and services and this production in turn produces a demand for capital goods; the production of both provides income, in the form of wages, rents and dividends for consumers. At the same time the government claims taxes from both producers and consumers while also itself demanding goods and providing income. By these means existing systems of human activities are kept running.

Changes in the pattern of activities are, however, brought about by another process. Not all consumer income is spent, nor is all production profit distributed as income. Some of both is retained as savings and this ultimately finds its way as investment in production to create new capital assets of plant,* buildings† or vehicles.[8] Most fundamental changes in the pattern of activities are associated with capital investments. In principle capital investment in plant, buildings or vehicles is intended to serve some possibly impending change in activities. In practice it is both cause and consequence of such changes. The road is built to accommodate the increasing demand for movement and itself generates that demand; shortening of working hours both necessitates and is enabled by an increasing reliance on machinery to maintain output. In these ways activity changes are inextricably linked with the allocation of capital resources.

Of the three kinds of capital asset which investment creates, buildings are the most important in value terms. Table 1.2 shows that nearly two-thirds of the existing capital stock and about half of the gross annual capital formation by value is in the form of buildings. Plant and vehicles are relatively more important in the replacement element of capital formation. Table 1.3 showing the percentage rate of replacements and net additions to gross

* Including both plant and machinery.
† Including both building and works.

TABLE 1.2. U.K. GROSS CAPITAL STOCK AND CAPITAL FORMATION 1970[1]

	Gross capital stock £ millions %		Gross capital formation £ millions %		Net addition element £ millions %		Replacement element £ millions %	
Vehicles	8800	7	809	12	199	6	610	19
Plant	41,600	30	2713	39	1224	33	1489	46
Buildings	87,600	63	3364	49	2250	61	1114	35
Total	138,000	100	6886	100	3673	100	3213	100

Note: [1] At 1963 prices.
Source: derived from Central Statistical Office (1972), *National Income and Expenditure 1971,* H.M.S.O., London, tables 54, 62 and 65.

TABLE 1.3. U.K. CAPITAL FORMATION AS % OF GROSS CAPITAL STOCK 1970[1]

	Gross capital formation	Net addition element	Replacement element
Vehicles	9.2%	2.3%	6.9%
Plant	6.5%	3.0%	3.5%
Buildings	3.8%	2.5%	1.3%

Note: [1] At 1963 prices.
Source: derived from Central Statistical Office (1972), *National Income and Expenditure 1971,* H.M.S.O., London, tables 54, 62 and 65.

capital stock explains why this is so. While the rates of net additions to the existing stock for all three kinds of asset are comparable at 2–3% of the value of the existing stock, the replacement rate varies from 1.3% for buildings through 3.5% for plant to 6.9% for vehicles. From this it is evident that vehicles and plant have shorter lives than buildings; at these replacement rates vehicles have average lives of about 15 years, plant about 30 years and buildings about 80 years. The significance of these differences is in the related differing propensity of activity system changes to be associated with capital investment in the different classes of asset. The lower replacement rate of buildings suggests that many activity changes will occur without substantial capital investment in building and that buildings will become adapted, at

TABLE 1.4. U.K. CAPITAL FORMATION BY ACTIVITY GROUP[1] 1970[2]

	Vehicles £ millions %		Plant £ millions %		Buildings £ millions %		Total £ millions %	
Housing	—	—	—	—	1465	34	1465	17
Services	325	33	630	18	634	15	1589	18
Social Welfare	27	3	164	5	624	14	815	9
Utilities	11	1	474	14	434	10	919	10
Transport	465	47	411	12	621	14	1497	17
Manufacturing	123	12	1595	46	419	10	2137	24
Agriculture	29	3	101	3	112	3	242	3
Mining	7	1	125	3	14	0	146	1
Total	987	100	3500	100	4323[3]	100	8810[3]	100

Source: derived from Central Statistical Office (1972), *National Income and Expenditure 1971,* H.M.S.O., London, table 57.

Notes: [1] The activities in this table are groupings of the classes used in the source, as follows:

Housing   =dwellings.
Services   =construction; wholesaling; retailing; insurance, banking, finance and business services; other transport and services.
Social Welfare =education; health; welfare.
Utilities   =gas; electricity; water, sewerage and land drainage.
Transport   =railways; road passenger transport; shipping; harbours, docks and canals; air transport; postal, telephone and radio communications; roads and car parks.
Manufacturing=total manufacturing.
Agriculture   =agriculture; forestry; fishing.
Mining   =coal mining; other mining and quarrying.

[2] At current prices.
[3] Less transfer costs of land and buildings.

low capital cost, to accommodate new activity systems. This is clearly known to be the case. In contrast, the investment in vehicles and plant associated with activity system changes more frequently involves substantial renewal of capital assets. In all cases some of the replacement of capital stock will represent a straightforward replacement of worn out stock by stock of the same nature in order to continue serving the same activity, albeit with better performance. Thus only a proportion of the replacement element of the gross capital formation is bound up with changes in activities, systems, whereas all the net addition element will be.

The pattern of investment in different activity systems differs greatly between the types of asset, as Table 1.4 shows. Investment in vehicles is heavily concentrated in the transport sector and the services sector, the latter largely due to wholesaling and retailing, and to a lesser extent in the manufacturing sector but with little elsewhere. Investment in plant is heavily weighted towards the manufacturing sector, supplemented by the services, utilities and transport sectors. Investment in buildings is most strongly represented in the housing sector, but has a wider spread across other sectors than either vehicles or plant.

Taking total investment in all assets manufacturing is clearly dominant, accounting for almost one-quarter of the total. Next in importance come services 18%, housing 17%, and transport 17%. The latter two comprise rather diverse activities especially transport which comprises land, sea and air transport; land transport alone represents about 7% of total investment. Next in importance come utilities 10%, social welfare 9% and finally, and fairly insignificantly, agriculture 3% and mining 1%. From this it is apparent that the big changes in activity systems associated with investment are in the activities of residence and production of goods and services.

ENVIRONMENTS

Table 1.2 illustrates the preponderance of buildings among both the existing stock of capital assets and gross and net capital formation. The community has more capital tied up in and puts more investment into buildings than into plant or vehicles. But building makes claims not just on resources of capital; it also makes substantial claims on land resources. And it is largely through the allocation of land to activities and the use of capital to adapt that land by constructional works that the environment of cities, towns and countryside is changed.

The physical environment has a number of aspects. It provides firstly unique locations in space for particular human activities. Activity systems extend through space and spatial interaction between activity locations is therefore an important dimension of activity systems. In these terms between-place activities and within-place activities can be distinguished.[9] The former are communication activities by which volumes of information, money, materials, goods and persons are transferred from one location to another: transport, telecommunications, waste discharges are activities of this kind. The latter, within-space activities, are located at points in space at which goods are produced or consumed: manufacturing, recreation, residence are activities of this kind. The two kinds of activities and their locations are of course related and mutually supportive. Each could not be sustained without the other, for the activities of production and consumption needs continuous supply and removal of materials and goods as much as communications are generated by production and consumption.

These systems of located activities function within spaces adapted to provide accommodation. These include dwellings, roads, railways, factories, parks, seashores, pipelines, forests, airfields, quarries and so on, representing a variety of ways in which physical spaces have been adapted to better accommodate the pursuit of activities. The form of adaptation also relates closely to the intensity of the activity. For within-space activities intensity is normally measured in relation to space—persons per acre, sales per square foot, for example—whereas for between-place activities it is frequently measured in relation to time—gallons per day, vehicles per hour, for example. Generally the greater the intensity of activities, the more elaborate and capital intensive the adaptation of space will be.

This adaptation of space not only provides accommodation for the activities. It is also the process by which the external environment changes, in particular in terms of its sentient qualities of appearance, sound and smell. Buildings, constructions, surfaces and planting are the visual elements which make up the man-made townscape and landscape of the environment. At the same time the activities themselves, particularly through discharge of their wastes, can have a direct impact on the external environment, extending beyond visual to aural and olfunctory impacts in the form of land dereliction, air and water pollution and noise. These qualities are as much characteristics of the physical environment as buildings themselves.

It is as difficult to put some statistical measure on the prevalence of different environments as with life styles. Land use, although a fairly narrow and imprecise indicator of environmental conditions in the general sense, is the nearest proxy. But even data on land use is scarce. Nationally the balance of broadly defined land uses is as shown in Table 1.5. Agricultural land use, and hence rural environments, predominate as would be expected. Nor is this balance changing very rapidly. In the post-war period the annual

TABLE 1.5. LAND USE IN GREAT BRITAIN 1960

Agriculture	82.4%
Forest and woodland	7.4%
Urban and other uses	10.2%

Source: Best, Robin H. (1968) Competition for land between rural and urban uses, in: *Land Uses and Resources: Studies in Applied Geography*, Inst. of Brit. Geog., London.

national conversion of land from agricultural to urban uses has been about 0.1% of the total land each year and there has been a comparable conversion rate to forest and woodland.[10] It has been estimated that urban needs in the next 40 years can be met with a slightly lower rate of conversion of agricultural land.[11] Regionally conversion rates have varied around this national average, having been greatest in the London region and the urban regions of the Midlands and the North. This slow but steady increase in urban land use is the product of both population growth and migration and the provision of new and renewed accommodation for activities at markedly lower densities than have been common hitherto. The extension of the urban environment is therefore associated with a change in its nature and appearance.

Within the urban areas evidence suggests that processes of change move towards, in broad terms, a density of about 30 hectares/1000 persons including all urban uses like housing, open space, industry, schools, shops, offices, public buildings and transport—reducing to this in redeveloping areas, increasing to this in newly developing areas.[12] Similar processes account for reductions in density in larger towns and cities as they redevelop and increases in density in smaller towns as they expand. But it is still true, in general, that the larger the urban area, the higher its density. Table 1.6 shows that these variations in overall density are mirrored in the densities of individual land uses. In urban areas of all sizes housing is the dominant land use, and consequently residential areas the predominant environment, comprising half the urban area. Next in importance is open space, more apparent in smaller urban areas than in larger. Industry, education and other uses are of lesser importance.

Just as much change in activities occurs without making additional investment demands on capital or altering life styles for the population, so much

TABLE 1.6. PATTERNS OF LAND USE IN URBAN AREAS, ENGLAND AND WALES

	Average popula-tion	hectares/1000 persons					
		Total urban area	Hous-ing	Indus-try	Open space	Educa-tion	Other
County boroughs	168,000	17.5	7.6	1.4	3.3	0.5	4.7
Large towns	31,700	29.8	12.6	2.3	6.1	1.0	7.8
Small towns	4700	34.0	16.2	1.7	10.5	1.1	4.5

Source: Best, Robin H. (1968) Competition for land between rural and urban uses, in: *Land Uses and Resources: Studies in Applied Geography*, Inst. of Brit. Geog., London.

activity change makes little additional claim on land resources or makes much impact on the physical environment. But where changing activities are restricted by existing locations, accommodations or environments, there can be two environmental consequences: locational change or develop-mental change.[13] Locational change occurs when activities seek different, more suitable spaces in which to accommodate themselves. This may mean a change of site or a change of route: for example, the relocation of a distribu-tion depot or the rerouteing of a bus line. Through such changes the activity's locational relationships with other activities are altered, presum-ably improved. Developmental change occurs when building or engineering works are undertaken to adapt and modify spaces to better accommodate an activity. Again it may be site development or network development; for example, the rehabilitation of a housing area or the construction of a bypass. Through such change the accommodation provided for activities is changed. Through both kinds of change alterations to the sentient environment will be brought about. The two kinds of change are frequently alternatives. Relocations occur because existing sites or routes cannot be developed further or because existing building stocks are so run down that relocation rather than on site renewal is a financially viable action. But they can also be related, for relocating activities commonly require development to accom-modate them at new locations, and activities expanding by developing existing sites or routes frequently displace other activities which must then relocate.

SYSTEMIC CHANGE

The relationships between activities and human, capital and land resources produce in these ways changes in life styles, investments and environments. These changes are themselves characteristically interactive, continuous and marginal. They are *interactive* because the resources and activities are related in a system in which all elements have the potential for interaction with all others.[14] The total activity-resource system is itself composed of three subsystems of life styles, investments and environments, focused principally on the interactions between activities and one particular resource. These subsystems will exhibit particularly intense interactions within them in which changes in any one of the elements can alter the state of the subsystem and cause a response in another element. But the sub-systems will also exhibit interactions between themselves, albeit of a lower intensity. Thus, for example, the decay of some industrial building stock forces the industrialist to consider new capital investments which he decides are best made at a different location, meaning a rundown in local employment providing the opportunity for redeveloping the site for housing, but with a severe consequent reduction of job opportunities, loss of income and a change in the life style of the local population.

Through such interactions, change in the system becomes *continuous*. Any static conception of the interrelationships between activities themselves and between activities and resources and of the nature of the resulting life styles, investment patterns and environments is an abstraction. The system is so dynamic and interconnected that the alteration of one element immediately acts to evoke alterations in others, perhaps in a great many others. In this way chain reactions are set up through the system as a whole. The speed and range of reaction will differ in different parts of the system. For example, changes in job opportunities have already been noted as fundamental to life style changes through income levels and social status; again, the slow replacement rate for building assets as compared to plant and vehicles indicates a constraint on the speed of some environmental adaptations to change; or again, the preponderance of housing as an element in urban environments means that a change affecting housing accommodation will have a widespread effect on towns and cities. Within the system and subsystems there will be relationships of these kinds which can speed or restrain reactive changes as well as relationships which diversify or confine them. So that change, while continuous, will in places be fast, in others slow, in some respects spreading wider and wider, in others narrowing down.

But although continuous, change is still *marginal*. At any one point in time, the system and its subsystems are fairly stable. The changes which occur and are so evident are really marginal increases or decreases in the elements. From one year to the next the shift in capital allocation between sectors or between assets is normally quite slight. In any one year only small percentages of land uses are being changed or small pockets of the environment remade. Equally over short time periods only tiny proportions of the population significantly change their socio-economic status or life style. Only in those circumstances in which system interactions are so intense that widespread changes are occurring at relatively rapid rates do the system and subsystems begin to change in more than marginal ways. This can happen but is usually confined severely in space and time. It happens, for example, with a large-scale redevelopment scheme, or with the increased wealth in a subregion from newly discovered mineral resources, or with a sudden collapse in the economic base of a locality through changed market conditions for its goods. But such effects are infrequent, not least because the community strives purposefully to avoid them by such devices as phasing development programmes, taxing new adventitious sources of wealth to spread the benefits more widely and cushioning households against income loss from unemployment. Over longer periods of time the elements in the system will change in their entirety but mostly through a succession of marginal, incremental changes.

Such interactive, continuous, marginal change of this kind is best described as systemic change[15] to indicate its boundlessness through all the subsystems and through time and space. It is in these processes of systemic change that public administration intervenes to secure ends that unimpeded changes would not themselves secure—to provide needed goods and services, to minimise social disbenefits and maximise social benefits, to lessen constraints on private action by underwriting risks or mediating conflicts, to protect the community from self-injurious actions and conserve its assets for the future. All these rationales for public intervention to control systemic change can find some application in the life style, investment and environment subsystems.

In this way there are three broad spheres of public action; those of social affairs, economic affairs and environmental affairs. Social affairs is concerned essentially with public actions to assist the realisation of human potential, through the physical and intellectual development of individuals and the social development of families and communities. Education, health, social welfare, income support, job creation and training are all examples of public action within this sphere, principally directed to changes in life styles. Economic affairs is concerned essentially with public actions to secure the best utilisation of capital resources by directing them to activities which will create the greatest wealth and satisfaction for the community. Demand management, investment incentives, research and development support, interurban transport are examples of public actions coming in this sphere and directed principally to investment changes. Environmental affairs is concerned essentially with public actions to conserve and develop land, air and water resources to serve both economically productive and other human activities.[16] Housing development and improvement, land use control, pollution control, landscape conservation are examples of public actions within this sphere directed principally towards environmental change.

Planning as a field of public administration falls within the sphere of environmental affairs. Its institutions, its powers, its typical programmes of action, its associated technical skills and ideologies are focused on the understanding and control of environmental change within the context of systemic change as a whole. And as it becomes harder to disentangle one kind of environmental change from another, as the relationships between the elements in the environmental system become increasingly close and increasingly perceived as close, then planning and environmental policy become almost synonymous.

CHAPTER 2

Forces of Environmental Change

THESE processes of systemic environmental change whereby activities themselves occur and recur and land resources become committed to them, with or without public control, are brought about by the actions of various agents. Their actions are purposive, that is, they are motivated by the prospect of some reward or the threat of some sanction. These rewards and sanctions comprise the system of incentives which provide the driving force behind environmental change.

Among these agents a distinction can be made between those belonging to the community and those belonging to its government. By government is meant the elected central and local authorities which exert measures of control over the pursuit of activities and whose locus in this rests essentially on the law. By community is meant the households, firms and institutions which are engaged in activities providing and consuming goods and services of various kinds, subject to control by the government. This is not a clear-cut distinction, principally because both central and local government themselves engage in the production and consumption of goods and services directly or indirectly.

Both the agents within the community and those within government are responsive to incentive systems. But in relation to the public authorities' action to control systemic environmental change, these incentive systems are both a guide and a constraint. The incentives to which the community agents respond provide a guide to the sort of interventions which will most effectively secure desirable directions of change, while the incentives to which the government agents respond provide a constraint, whether statutory or electoral or financial, on the kinds of intervention they can pursue.

The agents of change in the community are operators, developers and consumers and the main government agents are local government and central government. Operators, for example, retailers, manufacturers, transport

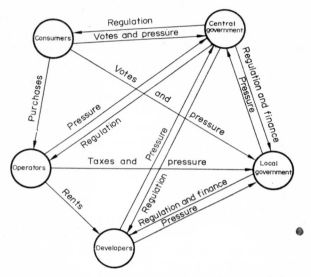

FIG. 2.1. Incentive systems motivating environmental change.

operators, school authorities, insurance companies, landlords provide goods and services in the widest sense. Developers provide the fixed building stock, and to a lesser extent the less fixed plant and vehicles, with which goods and services are produced. Consumers take the products of operators' activities and so keep the operators in business. Local government acts both to promote and regulate change by developers and operators. Central government's controls are more diverse: some are exercised over local authorities; some are exercised directly or indirectly over consumers, operators and developers.

The direction and nature of the influence of these agents on each other are illustrated in Fig. 2.1. These patterns of influence represent elements in the system of incentives to which the agents of change respond. Potentially there can be two-way influences between each pair of all five agents, providing twenty interactions in all. But of these only fourteen would seem significant as rewards or sanctions motivating actions which produce environmental change. In these fourteen interactions, the nature of the main influence exerted differs between financial transactions, political influence and statutory regulation. Financial transactions include the payment of rent by operators to developers, the payment of purchase prices by consumers to operators, the payment of taxes to government and the payment by government of financial assistance through loans and grants. Political influence includes formal electoral influence by consumers' votes for central and local government as well as informal pressure by all community agents on government and by local government on central government. Statutory regulation is exclusively a sanction of government, both central and local, and is exercised in different ways over consumers, operators and developers and by central over local government. These are the three kinds of incentives motivating relations between the five agents of environmental change.

OPERATORS

Operators occupy a key position for the activities which they operate are the reason for much of the rest, providing as they do both the goods and services the community demands and the income from employment needed to sustain that demand. One consumer's purchases provide another man's income in the continuous chain of production and consumption. In such a consumer society the operators are central—the providers of capital and consumer goods (manufacturers), retail goods and services (retailers), accommodation (landlords), learning (educational authorities), transport (highway and public transport authorities and goods vehicle operators), health (social welfare agencies), entertainment and so on.

Operators are very diverse. They include both private and public sector agents. The private sector operators range from single individuals, such as self-employed farmers or shopkeepers, to large corporations employing thousands, run by professional managers and owned by shareholders. Private sector agents dominate as operators manufacturing goods, providing services and operating part of the housing stock. The public sector operators include central government which has limited but specific duties as an operator, including running the defence system as well as general administrative responsibilities, and local government with a greater range of duties as an operator including frequently the transport system, the education system, part of the housing system and the social welfare system. The public sector also includes a large variety of public corporations such as electricity and gas undertakings, passenger transport authorities and regional hospital boards.

Operators differ also in whether they function by providing private or public goods and services. Private goods and services are those for which the seller can fairly simply and equitably calculate a price. Public goods and services are those for which the seller cannot do this simply or equitably. Almost without exception the private sector operators are concerned with providing private goods and services whereas public sector agencies are concerned with providing either private or public goods and services.

Even more important in understanding the motivation of operators is the distinction between remunerative and non-remunerative operations. Remunerative operations include all private sector operations and some public sector operations providing private goods. Incomings from remunerative operations must at least cover outgoings, although the actual definition of incomings and outgoings and the exact nature of the desired relationship between them will vary between cases. Some private sector agencies may seek to maximise profit, some public sector agencies may be concerned only to break even. There will also be other objectives not of a narrowly financial nature which are important in influencing the month by month and year by year running of an operator's business.[1] Non-remunerative operations include the provision of public goods and a number of private goods which, for various reasons, it has been decided by the community should be collectively financed. Increasingly operators in this field seek to demonstrate that the social benefits provided by their goods and services have a notional monetary value in excess of the outgoings. The basic calculation is therefore the same as for remunerative operations but there are difficulties in both identifying the relevant social costs and benefits and in finding acceptable monetary values for them. Where incomings in these terms are not definable then the rule relates commonly to the concept of standards of provision or performance to be maintained or improved.[2] Nevertheless, whatever the differences and difficulties in detail the basic modus operandi, the production of goods and services, and motivation, balancing of incomings and outgoings, are the same for a diversity of operators.

DEVELOPERS

Development in the widest sense is the process by which capital assets are created: buildings, plant and vehicles. It is with these assets that goods and services are produced. The creation of plant and vehicle assets is relatively simple, being itself a process of production with those assets as the goods produced. The creation of buildings and works—constructional assets—is far more complex due to the varied and unique characteristics of the land resource. It involves at least the following stages:[3]

    (i) assessment of demand for development;
    (ii) acquisition of interest in land;
    (iii) preparation of designs;
    (iv) arrangement of finance both short term and long term;
    (v) arrangement of construction and contracts;
    (vi) obtaining of public consents and permissions;
    (vii) construction;
    (viii) lease or sale and occupation.

Thereby many parties are involved—the original landowner, legal advisers, the developer himself, building contractors, public authorities, finance institutions, the operator who occupies the building. In particular developments more than one role may be played by one party: landowners who improve land with roads and sewers and leave plots to builders; firms which finance themselves the extension of their premises on land they already own; education authorities building schools with the help of central government finance. Developers are quite as diverse as operators.

Like operators they can also be divided between the public and the private sector. Among the public developers are central government departments, local authorities and public corporations of various kinds. Among private developers are private individuals, insurance companies, building contractors, private firms and companies, universities. Table 2.1 shows how capital investment in building is split between classes of developer.

The split between public and private sectors for all building is about half and half; for dwellings the public sector is more dominant. Central government is relatively unimportant as a developer, mostly confined to developments for defence, trunk roads and motorways, administration and the National Health Service. Local government is much more important with its house building, transport and social welfare and education developments. Public corporations are relatively less important. They include statutory undertakers, nationalised industries, Post Office and new town development corporations. Private development includes both personal investment, largely the purchase of new houses for owner-occupation, and company

TABLE 2.1. U.K. CAPITAL FORMATION[1] BY SECTOR 1970

	Dwellings	Other buildings and works
Private sector—personal	45%	10%
—companies	2%	32%
Public sector —public corporations	6%	13%
—central government	1%	16%
—local government	46%	29%
Total	100%	100%

Source: derived from Central Statistical Office (1972), *National Income and Expenditure 1971*, H.M.S.O., London, table 52.

Note 1 at current prices.

investment. It covers three main classes: housing development mostly built for sale, commercial developments for offices and shops and to a lesser extent warehousing, and industrial developments built largely by operators for their own occupation. Development as a whole is therefore dominated by private developers and local authorities which together provide 70% of all building and over 90% of all dwellings. The make up of the private and public sector development is then

PRIVATE SECTOR	PUBLIC SECTOR
Dwellings	Dwellings
Offices	Offices
Manufacturing	Defence
Retailing	Communications
	Utilities
	Social welfare and education

In carrying out developments the developer buys goods and services which enable the creation of a capital asset, but the goods and services provided with that asset in return, through occupation of the development only become available over its life. Development therefore necessitates investment funds which may be those of the developer himself, but more commonly the developer, both private and public, will borrow funds from others for the purpose of investment on payment of interest. The decision to develop to create capital assets is influenced by the relation between the rate of return on the development and the rate of interest on borrowed money.

While this is generally true, there are important differences between the calculations made by private and public developers because the kind of development and means of financing it differ. But, apart from these differences, there is also an important distinction between development, both public and private, carried out for operators' own occupation and that carried out by developers for sale or lease to operators. Very little public development is in fact carried out for sale so there are usually five kinds of development worth distinguishing:[4]

(i) *Private development for sale* represents the simplest case and is exemplified by private housing development. The developer is concerned, on the one hand, with capital costs and any interest payable on finance borrowed during the development period and, on the other, with the income from the sale of completed development.

(ii) *Private development for letting* differs from this in adding a continuing annual cost to the initial capital costs, again including interest payable on borrowed finance, to be set against the rental income from the development. This form of finance is common with much private development of offices and shops where insurance companies and pension funds and, to a lesser extent, property unit trusts and property bond funds are the source of finance.

(iii) *Private operators' own development*, of which the most notable kind is probably industrial development, again necessitates consideration of both capital and annual costs, but in this case the return is not directly a money yield, but rather a return in the form of the profits on increased production or sales which the new development makes possible. The main source of finance with this class of development is either companies' own accumulated reserves, the commercial banks or new share issues, supplemented in certain circumstances by government funds.

(iv) *Public development for lease* is exemplified by local authority housing, although remunerative local authority operations like car parks, markets and in cases central area developments can come in this class. Here the main costs are again capital and annual costs and the

income is from rents. The common sources of finance may be borrowing from the Public Works Loan Board or through the issue of local
authority stock or through mortgages, commonly supplemented by
specific capital or recurrent grants paid by central government as
well as the general rate support grant.

(v) *Public operators' own developments*, like roads, schools, libraries and
welfare, normally yield no money income to set against capital and
annual costs of the development. Instead there are social benefits of
health, amenity, saving of time and effort, literacy and numeracy
accruing to the consumer over the life of the development. Increasingly an attempt is made to devise monetary measures of the value of
these social benefits in order to reproduce for this class of development the relationship between the rate of interest and the rate of
return basic to development decisions in other classes. The sources
of finance are the same as for public development for letting.

CONSUMERS

While the activities of operators sustain those of developers, the foundation of the whole activity system lies in the propensity of the population to
consume.[5] The basic unit of consumption is the household, largely pooling
its income and expenditure and thereby sharing a similar pattern of consumption and life style. The four most important items of household
expenditure are:

(i) *Housing*—the acquisition through a mortgage or rental payments of
housing, not just the accommodation provided by the dwelling but
the entire housing package with its particular locational, environmental and status qualities;

(ii) *Retail goods and services*—ranging from necessities to luxuries of life
largely satisfying material wants and mostly acquired by purchase in
shops;

(iii) *Recreation*—increasingly important, extremely diverse, largely providing intellectual or sensory satisfactions;

(iv) *Transport*—either by private or public transport, in either case the
means of consuming goods and services available at different
locations.

But these four items do not cover the whole range of consumption for two main reasons. Firstly, there are a large range of goods and services which are not provided by operators in return for payments and not therefore the object of direct consumer expenditure. Most importantly there is a whole sector of consumption of social services, financed by taxation, which falls in this class. This needs adding—

(v) *Social Services*—including notably health, welfare and educational provision.

Secondly, it is necessary to regard employment as something which is consumed. Employment has the role of a factor of economic production in both operation and development. But equally employment is something which households require and consume, providing thereby the main source of income rather than an outlet for expenditure. So—

(vi) *Employment*—the principal means by which households gain income and sustain consumption.

It is through their employment that households are enabled to purchase, through taxes or direct payments, housing, retail goods and services, recreation, transport and social services, thus completing a circle of consumption which interacts with the activities of operators and through operators with developers.

The relationship of consumers to the other agents is not just passive. They do not accept any housing, goods, transport, or indeed employment which is offered. To a large extent a range of possibilities exist and, within the limits of skill, income, knowledge, taste and accessibility, the consumer exercises a choice. This is largely a market choice. The market is in many cases a true economic market as is largely the job market, the retail market, the recreation market and the transport market. This does not mean that there are perfect markets where demand and supply are exactly responsive to changes in each other, but for the most part price determines the allocation of goods and services to the consumer—the price a man can command for his labour, the price the household can afford for retail goods and so on. However, road space as a transport service is universal and freely available, as also are some recreation facilities. The housing market is only partly an economic market in that a substantial proportion of goods in the public housing sector are allocated to households on criteria other than the price they can pay. The social services market, excepting privately financed provision, is a noneconomic market, in which services are allocated according to administrative rules which relate to politically determined needs rather than economically determined demand. But whatever the difference between these markets, they all represent mechanisms by which individual consumers can bring pressure to bear directly on the operator supplying the particular goods and collectively these pressures can alter market conditions.

But this market power is not the sole influence in the hands of consumers. In a democracy with universal adult suffrage they possess also political power. They are thus able through the two remaining agents, local and central government, to exercise influence over the activities of operators and developers. The degree of influence depends on two crucial factors: the powers available to local and central government to control the activities of operators or developers and the means through which consumers can persuade governments to share their objectives. Governmental influence is very varied. In cases where government itself is the operator—as with most social services, some transport, housing and recreation services—influence over development and operation is clearly great; otherwise it is imperfect to varying degrees. Voting at elections is the most formal means of influencing governments, and elections, both national and local, are associated with campaigns to promote particular controls by elected governments. While important, this is by no means the sole or possibly the most important means of influence of the governed on governors. There is a continuing ebb and flow of pressure placed on government by particular groups of consumers, as also of operators and developers—at local government level amenity societies, parent–teacher associations, trade union branches, neighbourhood groups, sports clubs and so on; at central government level interest groups representing different sectors of the economy, groups from different parts of the nation, or simply groups sharing particular perspectives or priorities. The movement for more participatory government is an attempt to provide more formal opportunities for influences such as these, and also for the influence of consumers outside or unrepresented by such organisations to be brought to bear on government decisions.[6]

LOCAL GOVERNMENT

On the one hand local government responds politically to these consumer, operator and developer influences, on the other hand it has statutory duties

and is limited by its statutory powers, as well as by the finances and manpower it has available at any point in time.[7] Traditionally local authorities
have functioned within the sphere of environmental affairs by providing
certain services. But the existence of local *government*, as opposed to local
administration, means that it can adjust its actions to its own knowledge of
changing needs, problems and opportunities.[8] In this context, its use of
its powers, finances and manpower represent possible means to political
ends rather than simple duties. In practice local government performs in two
distinct ways in seeking to exercise control over environmental change.[9]
In some aspects it has a promotional role initiating changes; in other aspects
it has a regulatory role responding to changes initiated by others.

Its promotional role is largely determined by its range of activities as
developer and operator in its own right. Its powers in these respects are
mostly as a provider of social service facilities, some transport services and
utilities, some housing, and occasional involvement in town centre developments or cultural and recreational provision. But its promotional role is
frequently extended further by use of its influence or by use of financial
inducement. The exercise of influence is a very complex matter, but information and knowledge are crucial to operators, consumers and developers and
local authorities are large stores of information on past, present and future
situations. The finances available for promotion of either development or
operation by other agents are diverse—examples are house improvement
grants, community development project grants, conservation grants, loans
to housing associations and individual house buyers and so on. Local
authorities can also offer financial inducement through making land available
for development on favourable terms. Many authorities engage in property
acquisition and disposal, frequently on leasehold terms, particularly in town
centres but also increasingly for new residential or industrial development
as well. In cases the disposal terms are enhanced by the advance provision
of the site infrastructure of access roads, water and sewerage and power
supplies.

The regulatory role is also diverse in its applications. It exists in relation
to those kinds of environmental change which have been statutorily made
subject to approval by local authorities. The change may be subject to prior
permission from the authority or it may be subject to challenge by the
authority. Development control is the most widespread example of environmental regulation necessitating, with certain exceptions, permission for any

building works or change of land use. Other powers exist to regulate changes in the quality of accommodation in dwellings, offices, factories and other workplaces, and to require improvements where that accommodation falls below predefined standards; yet other powers exist for the regulation of industrial processes particularly from the viewpoints of public health and safety including, for example, restrictions on changes in noise levels, air emissions and water discharges; and traffic can also be subjected to a wide range of regulations.

In performing these promotional and regulatory roles the local authority is essentially in pursuit of its own political objectives, constrained by the statutory powers, finances and manpower at its command. All of these constraints can be lessened. The authority can seek by private bill procedures in Parliament or by influence exercised upon central government to secure changes in their statutory duties or obligations. The authority has discretion to increase the size and composition of its manpower. This action will have financial costs. Within the limits of its statutory powers financial constraints have the most significant effect on local government actions. As an operator or as a developer in particular fields it will be concerned to balance the books in the sense that incomings as rents and benefits are, in real or equivalent terms, at least equal to outgoings. But in the broader sense its actions will be constrained by the finances available to it. These come from three main sources: grants, loans and rate income. Grants from the central government are of two kinds. Firstly, there is the annual rate support grant paid to local authorities on the basis of a formula which reflects both the strength of their rate income base and their expenditure needs. Secondly, there are grants tied to particular programmes or projects and usually provided as an aid to capital investment. Central government grants are set at levels uninfluenced by individual local authorities acting collectively. Individual authorities can, however, make lesser or greater claims on what grants are available. Loans may be obtained by local authorities to finance capital expenditure where they are acting themselves as developers. The amount of borrowing will be principally limited by the proportions of current expenditure in succeeding years which can be set aside to make repayments. The balance of the local authority's finances must be met from rate income, through which consumers and operators are taxed on the basis of the value of the land and property they own. The local authority has complete discretion in fixing the level of local taxation in this way, but in practice consumer and operator influences on local government put firm limits on acceptable rate levels, although rate reductions for particular classes of property and the payment of rate rebates to particular classes of household exist to mitigate the impact of rates on domestic taxpayers.

In these ways there can be quite a close connection between the processes of environmental change and the financial resources of the local authority.[10] The total value of land and property which provide the tax base for its rates, the kinds of services of an environmental, social or economic kind which it provides in relation to the needs of the community, the effect of both of these on the level and availability of government grants are all matters which will be affected directly or indirectly by changes in the environment which the authority is seeking to promote or regulate. Its control must therefore be exercised with an eye both to improving the common welfare and to maintaining its financial viability.

CENTRAL GOVERNMENT

Behind local government as a promoter and regulator of environmental change stands central government. Its powers as developer and operator are fairly minimal, far less significant than those of the local authorities. Its powers of control over others' activities are greater but while pervasive—affecting developers, operators, consumers and local government alike—their impacts are frequently indirect and to some extent uncertain. For the most part central government actions have national or regional application to achieve consistency and equity. Its actions are inevitably therefore taken in some disregard of their impact on specific localities or specific groups, and can seem fairly blunt when applied to local environmental change.

Central government's role as manager of the national economy is clearly a fundamental influence on the actions of other agents. In addition to determining its own expenditures, it controls to varying degrees the capital and revenue expenditure of local authorities and public corporations. In particular, it regulates broadly the overall level of local government capital investment as well as the more specific investment programmes in certain sectors. Further, by adjusting the levels of national taxation, government loans and grants and by influencing credit terms, it affects developers' and operators' costs as well as the pattern of consumers' spending on goods and services. In consequence, it can influence the amount of savings that is possible out of consumers' or operators' incomes and so indirectly the availability of capital resources for investment and the attractiveness of competing investment opportunities. It can raise enough taxes to provide budget surpluses which can be used to finance capital investment for which there would otherwise have been insufficient savings. All these measures have effects on the incentive systems motivating environmental change.

These measures are, however, principally directed to the management of the national economy. Other central government actions fall within the spheres of social and environmental affairs. National actions within the social affairs sphere relating, for example, to the provision of education, health, social welfare or recreation facilities can affect the provision of goods and services to consumers and necessitate development to accommodate them, and in these ways affect environmental change.

More specific local impacts arise from action in the environmental affairs sphere. Central government accepts as a national political task some degree of direct control over environmental change. But for the most part this control is exercised through its influence over local authority's promotional and regulatory actions.[11] This influence is achieved either by financial inducement, regulation or exhortation. Its financial inducements to action are those grants which it makes available to local authorities, usually for capital investment: thus central government pays grants covering part of the cost of slum clearance, housing improvement, building conservation, derelict land reclamation, highway building, public transport improvements and some other capital works. Some grants are paid to local authorities themselves, some are channelled through local authorities and paid at their discretion to private operators and developers. Direct central government regulation of actions by local government is again principally tied to capital investment in the form of specific authorisations of individual projects which must be obtained from central government. The concern at this stage is not simply with the financial commitment implied by the project, but also with the priority being given to that project in relation to national needs and the technical adequacy of the proposal in terms of national policies. Little direct regulation of this kind is exercised by central government over private operators, developers or consumers. Two classes of exception are the permits needed for substantial new office or industrial development and the planning permissions granted or refused by central government when the application has been called in for their decision or referred to it on appeal from a local government decision.

As with local government, central government is acting to promote and regulate change in pursuit of its political objectives and subject to similar formal electoral sanctions and informal pressures from consumers, operators and developers. Unlike local government, however, central government's financial viability is not closely bound up with the direction of that change. And further unlike local government, in seeking to control change central government is not simply restricted to using the powers currently available to it for interventions through the system of incentives to which consumers, developers, operators and local government respond, but can through legislation seek directly to recast those powers to secure more effective control.

CHAPTER 3

Controlling Environmental Change

THE task of public administration is essentially to control processes of societal change, both by itself promoting changes or by regulating changes initiated by others. For environmental change responsibility for control is shared between central and local government, with the former defining through legal powers the context in which the latter operates, but with both levels exercising significant powers of controls over the activities of operators, developers and consumers. However, the leading role is that of the local authority. Even where situations arise which merit nationally or regionally consistent actions in response, the tendency in planning is for these responses to be administered by local government, acting partly as agent of central government for that purpose but also exercising local discretion in the precise application of the response. It is therefore the local authority which has the chief responsibility for controlling environmental change in the community, although at certain times, in certain places, in relation to certain kinds of change its locus as such may be limited or completely overridden by exercises of authority by others.

The local authority's efforts to control change will represent interventions in the activities of developers, operators or consumers to influence the system of incentives and sanctions within which they operate. Its *raison d'être* for such interventions lie entirely within the workings of the community, for the sole purpose of intervention is to establish relations and conditions more acceptable than the unimpeded working of the environment subsystem would itself produce. The planning objectives of a local authority should relate directly to their perception of the problems, needs and desires of the community it administers. It cannot exist to serve its own ends.

43

ACTION CYCLES

One way to represent this relationship between local government and the community is to conceive of it as a continuing dialogue in which messages— complaints, requests, demands, instructions, enactments, advice and so on —are passed back and forth between the parties.[1] The local authority and the community exist in this representation in their full diversity. The community embraces operators, developers and consumers within the area, both individually and as collectively organised in various groups and the same individuals and groups acting in different capacities—as employees, electors, landlords, shoppers, car drivers, parents and so on. Local government extends beyond its formal and legal aspects of council, committees and departments in a social, functional and political entity—the local politician can simultaneously be ward representative, party member and committee chairman, while the local authority professional may frequently owe allegiance to both the authority and his profession. There will also be cross-membership of community and government. All personnel in government are also members of the community, but more particularly a politician may be a landowner or a businessman, a professional may be an active member of some community group or political party. Many of these elements of diversity will have significance for the dialogue between the community and its government.

A round of dialogue is shown in Fig. 3.1 as an action cycle. It begins with a situation arising in the community which the local authority comes to perceive. It may be a change in the environment which has occurred or is in progress or is merely in prospect. In this latter case it may be more or less certain to occur. The situation is appraised by the authority to determine whether it raises issues which make a response possible or desirable and, if desirable, what choice of public actions are available and how they compare. The choice of action is made, the action is taken and, if effective, a change in the environment occurs to modify the original situation in the community. In this way one action cycle is completed.

This model of action cycles applies equally whether the authority is acting as a promoter or a regulator of change. The regulatory case can be illustrated by the process of development control. The situation arising in the community may be one in which a developer sees potential for providing additional office accommodation at low rents. It is straightforwardly per-

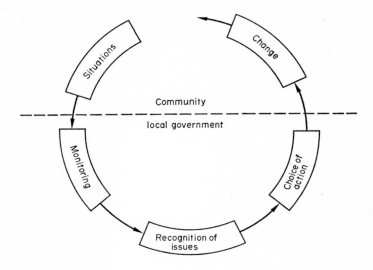

Fᴵɢ. 3.1. Simple action cycle.

ceived by the local authority by its receipt of a planning application to which it is statutorily obliged to respond. Within the limits of the powers available to it the choice of action for the authority is basically between refusal, approval or approval subject to conditions; additionally the local authority could seek to negotiate with the developer for the substitution of a new application closer to their wishes. A choice of action is made, for example, permission is granted, and in due course when the development is completed the original situation, the shortage of low-rent office accommodation, is changed. In such cases the roles of operators, consumers, developers, local and central government within the cycle are apparent: the operators lacking low-rent accommodation to let, the consumers demanding it, the developer providing it, the local authority permitting it with powers granted by central government. Another illustration, of a local authority in a promotional role, would be a situation involving a high accident record at a particular road junction where complex vehicular turning movements combine with busy pedestrian flows to and from a shopping parade. The situation might be perceived through police reports or complaints from the public. In this case the decision to respond or not is at the discretion of the authority. If it feels that issues are raised which merit response, the choice of action lies between securing some police regulation of traffic, improving carriageway marking or signals, redesigning the layout of the junction or rerouteing the traffic or pedestrian flows by traffic management or new road construction. After consideration a choice is made, action taken and, if it proves effective, conditions at the junction are changed.

Clearly in these cases the changes produced by these interventions do not just modify existing situations, but will themselves be generators of new situations in the future. Some of these may be foreseen at the time of the decision on appropriate actions in response to the original situation, some may be unforeseen. In the first illustration these further situations might be additional parking demands, new job opportunities, changes in the townscape arising from the office development. In the latter illustration there might be changes in travel patterns, possibly increases in accidents elsewhere, worsened access problems for shop deliveries and perhaps ultimately a loss of trade for the shopping parade. In these ways change in the environment is continuous and takes on the characteristics of systemic change. The dialogue between the community and its government becomes endless as action cycle follows action cycle, with new situations continuously arising in the community, being perceived by the authority, and facing it with choices on whether it can or should respond and, if so, what regulatory or promotional actions or interventions to make.

MONITORING THE ENVIRONMENT

That the local authority comes to perceive a situation existing or arising in the community environment which might call for its intervention is an outcome of its operations for systematically scanning that environment and recording changes in its condition. The operation of scanning is the function of the local authority's monitoring system; the operation of recording is the function of the local authority's information system. Any administration requires a flow of data on changes occurring external to itself. Its needs are not just for "hard" data on the state of the environment, mostly statistically recorded facts about, for example, population composition, building stocks or pollution levels. It also needs "soft" data indicating less certain knowledge about changes which seem likely, attitudes and intentions of developers, operators or consumers which are yet tentative, impressions of trends which seem to be developing though for the present they cannot be firmly charted in "hard" data. "Soft" data can be as valuable an indication of the state of the environment as "hard" data though inevitably it requires more circumspection in its use.[2]

Local authorities draw "hard" and "soft" data from four main sources: published data; unpublished data from within the authority or from central government; *ad hoc* surveys; correspondence and meetings and other direct observations.[3] All four sources have their strengths and weaknesses. The quinquennial and decennial censuses of the Office of Population Census and Surveys are preeminent as published sources for detailed local data; other national surveys like the Family Expenditure Survey and the General Household Survey are less useful locally. Unpublished data falls into two groups: data generated within the authority, especially records of executive decisions and actions such as planning permissions, building completions, rateable values, housing rents, and data from central government sources such as employment data from Department of Employment records and special tabulations of the census. For the most part both these sources yield "hard" data. *Ad hoc* surveys are necessary where ready collected data is either not available in sufficient detail or is in unusable form: examples of "hard" data might be land use data, income data, noise-level data, whereas examples of "soft" data might be from surveys of community attitudes, employers' intentions or expert forecasts. Correspondence, meetings and observations yield mostly "soft" data of a fairly unsystematic but nevertheless frequently very relevant kind. From this variety of sources the local authority is continuously exposed to data about the past, present and possible future state of the community and its environment.

But raw data by itself is of little use to the authority. Data is turned into information by processes of selection, aggregation and classification which give it meaning and relevance to its user. Information is relevant data. Monitoring will be drawing only relevant data from the four sources for storage in the information system. But further than that an effective monitoring system will seek to define significant indicators of the state of the environment which demonstrably mirror change in a variety of environmental variables.[4] Such indicators will be a principal means of reducing the otherwise bewildering variety of information yielded by monitoring the environment.

But the effectiveness of monitoring systems in producing useful information is constrained by data availability at its source, particularly its range, its level of detail and its periodicity. Some kinds of environmental change in the community are normally well documented in one or other of the four sources: examples are changes in traffic conditions, population numbers; unemployment rates. Others are frequently scarcely documented at all in any systematic way: examples are changes in property prices, changes in pollution levels, changes in the socio-economic structure of populations. Again, data may be available for a variable of interest but not in detailed enough form to be useful. Published and frequently unpublished survey data rarely relate to the individual person, household, business or property for which it was collected. Rather it is available in more generalised form either to preserve confidentiality or to increase intelligibility or to maintain statistical reliability where it has been collected by sample. The generalisation of the data may relate to areal units or categories of one kind or another: roads, enumeration districts, administrative areas on the one hand, socio-economic groups, Standard Industrial Classification classes, household types, land uses on the other. There is also frequently a time lag between data collection and its publication after processing. Data even where available will therefore always tend to be somewhat out of date. But more significant are the varying time intervals adopted by data collection agencies for updating information. Some data, particularly that flowing from executive decision making within the local authority, may be continuously becoming available and so updated; other data may be updated yearly, for example, population estimates, employment data, frequently traffic counts; census data is now updated quinquennially by the sample census and decennially by the full census; some sources, especially *ad hoc* surveys, may be updated only occasionally.

In these ways the local authority's state of knowledge about the community and its environment is continuously supplemented by its monitoring system and recorded in its information system. In terms of the action cycle, the information system represents a store to which successive cycles add information through monitoring operations and from which they withdraw information for use in deciding whether to respond to situations the authority faces and, if so, what choice of action to make. It exists therefore, as Fig. 3.2 illustrates, in the form of a loop off the main action cycle with a two-way linkage to it, both fed by and feeding the action cycle.

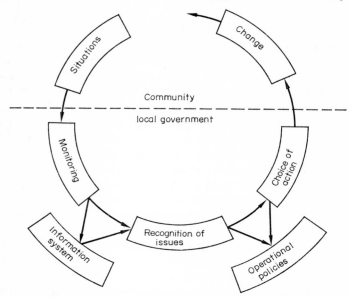

F IG. 3.2. Simple action cycle with information system and operational policies.

But thie information system does not exist independently of the local authority's attitude to change in the community, its value system. The information system must always be responding in some measure to the value system since the criterion of relevance which determines the inclusion of data in the former can only derive from the latter. Which characteristics of the environment are monitored depends on the theories which are believed to best explain the workings of the systems they belong to and best reflect the attitudes and preferences that the local authority holds.[5] At the same time, the local authority's factual knowledge will constrain and condition its values. Over time they will tend to monitor the variables which appear significant to them and neglect those seemingly of little or no significance. But what they consider significant will inevitably be influenced by the facts at their disposal. The authority's perception of environmental change yielded by its monitoring system and on which it must base its choice of responses and actions is therefore partly an expression of the facts available to it and partly an expression of the values it holds.

THE RECOGNITION OF ISSUES

The processes by which the local authority comes to recognise that situations existing or arising in the environment raise issues to which it should respond are more diverse and obscure than those by which it merely remains informed. What turns a situation into an issue is an acceptance by the local authority, or initially by those seeking to influence the authority to take action, that it is a matter to which they should respond. Issues are frequently characterised as problems and the local authority's response as a solution to that problem. But they can equally take the positive as well as the negative form and appear as opportunities to be grasped and exploited.

Clearly some messages coming from the community to the authority demand their response. Most evident in this class are formal applications for decisions and actions to which the authority must by statute respond; applications for permissions or for payments of grants, loans or rebates of various kinds are the prime examples. Another class of matters are brought to the attention of the authority by individuals or groups in the community seeking by political pressure to raise issues and secure actions by the local authority to meet their ends. Such initiatives may come from formal organisations like amenity societies, chambers of commerce or sports clubs, or from informal groups of neighbours, landowners, or traders temporarily banded together for this purpose. Such community pressure is frequently accompanied and sustained by publicity arranged through public meetings, petitions, press coverage and advertising, and takes on the form of an organised campaign to influence the authority.

Apart from these two classes in which the initiative comes principally from the community, there is a third class of issue in which the initiative and pressure come from the other direction, from central government. Here the local authority responds to situations identified as issues by central government through the imposition of statutory duties on the authority or through advice and exhortation, sometimes backed by the granting or withholding of finance or authorisation.[6] Some examples of statutory duties relate to the provision of sites for gypsy accommodation,[7] the closure of unfit houses,[8] and the maintenance of rural footpaths and bridleways.[9] Some examples of advice relate to the control of development on the coastline,[10] the minimisation of noise nuisance,[11] the location of new shopping centres[12] and the conservation of historic buildings.[13] These are all cases where central government is seeking to influence the response of local authorities to situations arising in the community.

There are yet other classes of situation which the authority recognises as issues on its own initiative and to which it responds, within the constraints of its powers, finances and manpower, at its own discretion. Behind these recognitions and responses lie the dispositions of both the professionals and the politicians in local government towards the needs of the community and the role of local government in meeting those needs.[14] The recognition of need implies the existence of opinions about desirable levels of provision and about the scale and quality of existing services. It is this view of the desirable which when measured against the existing situation determines the level of need. Professional officials in particular are strongly motivated by this aspect since their recognition of need is also a justification for their professional values and a determinant of expansion and development of their sphere of work. Need will also vary in scope, occurring either throughout the community or restricted to some areas or groups within it. If the scope is restricted to some areas or groups then attitudes towards those groups or areas assume significance and traditional identifications between political parties and community groups and the territorial basis of electoral representation encourage the existence of such attitudes. Such attitudes are probably most relevant to the motivation of politicians. Once the needs are perceived, attitudes towards the legitimacy of government intervention to meet those needs are important. These rest on the view taken of the proper balance between public and private action and implicit in this view is usually an attitude towards local government finance and particularly the level of local rates. Professionals will in general tend to be interventionist, again as an outcome of professional self-justification, while politicians will be more or less interventionist dependent on prevailing political doctrine. These dispositions in the local authority are essentially reflections of professional and political ideologies.[15]

There are then these five reasons why local authorities come to recognise issues arising in the community and to accept a case for their intervention: statutory obligation to respond, pressure from the community, pressure from central government, professional ideology or political ideology. These are not clear cut and mutually exclusive and in facing any situation it is likely that more than one reason will be applicable, maybe reinforcing each other, maybe conflicting. In particular the availability of powers is a basic requisite. Further, the local authority will always be operating within a general climate of opinion which is itself an expression of the disposition among the community at large to recognise issues and accept actions. This climate of opinion, frequently hard to define and in a state of continual flux, can find tangible expression in electoral behaviour. So that, amorphous as it is, it will always be a benchmark to which the decision to respond to environmental change must be related.[16]

THE CHOICE OF ACTION

Once an issue has been recognised and accepted by the local authority, it must decide on an action or intervention to control the situation. In principle the choice it faces is between promotional actions, initiating change as an operator or developer in its own right, or regulatory actions, using its powers to regulate operations or developments initiated by others. In practice its choice might combine both kinds of action. The range of its discretion in choosing an appropriate action will vary greatly with the situations it faces.[17] In some cases the alternative possibilities may be numerous, in others they may be so constrained by the available powers, finances and manpower to be very few in number. In a complex instance, for example, in responding to the issues raised by the prospective closure of a major indust-rial enterprise there may be many dimensions to the situation, the alterna-tives for action in relation to each dimension may be numerous, the relation-ships between these alternatives may be complex. In consequence the level of discretion is high and selection of a preferred set of responses may require a good deal of careful consideration. At the other extreme, for example, in dealing with applications for house improvement grants there will be less discretion since the statute itself defines some of the considerations, namely, the likely life of the property, the kind of work to be done, the proportion of the cost to be reimbursed, which govern the choice of action.[18]

But within whatever range of discretion, the local authority will be making a choice which is purposive, that is, directed towards its political objectives for the community. This can be true of any individual decision taken in isolation. But decisions like these rarely stand in isolation. The information available about situations in the community influences the values held regarding such situations and vice versa. Each choice of action and the consequential change in the community environment enters that store of information and thereby becomes an influence on the values which are brought to bear on succeeding choices of action.[19] In this way past decisions become potent influences on present choices and present decisions will have influence on future choices, without there being necessarily any commitment on the part of those deciding to act otherwise than by regarding each choice of action in isolation and considering each case on its merits.

In practice two other considerations reinforce this tendency towards consistency and regularity in the choice of action in response to similar situations, consistency as between choices and regularity over time. These are considerations of equity and effectiveness. The actions chosen by the authority represent sanctions or rewards for consumers, operators or developers seeking to change the environment in some way. By these actions individuals or groups in the community have their material or non-material satisfactions, for example, of income, aesthetic enjoyment, convenience or choice, enhanced or diminished in varying degrees. Basic to democratic political ideology is a concern that such government interventions should not be inequitable, in the sense of benefiting or disbenefiting one individual or group more or less than another in comparable situations. This search for equity imposes a consistency requirement on the choice of action. The search for effectiveness imposes both consistency and regularity requirements. Individual choices and actions may be purposive but, except where they are of a very major kind, they will rarely in themselves be sufficient to achieve the purposes or objectives of the authority. These can be approached or achieved only by successive actions, each representing a marginal change but incrementally adding up to something more significant. This is the nature of systemic change.* Successive choices must therefore be consistent so that through such regularity the choices of action can be not just individually but collectively purposive and effective.

In these ways, both by implicit processes and by explicit intention, the choices of action in response to similar situations arising independently in the community become consistent and regular and expressive of prevailing political values. Such situations become identifiable by attributes taken to typify classes of similar situations. So that for such classes of situation the choice of action can be indicated by conventions related to whatever characteristic attribute of the situation is considered important. Thus the choice of action stage in the action cycle may normally follow a course determined by

* See Chapter 2.

a generic viewpoint—a viewpoint for dealing with that class of situation. These viewpoints may be expressed in the local authority in the laying down of formal instructions, in general statements of intent or simply in the growth of conventions reflecting the perspective and experience of those concerned in making such decisions. But whatever the form, however formally or informally expressed, however general or specific, these viewpoints represent the operational policies of the local authority and the choices that are made on the basis of these policies are executive decisions.[20]

Thus a distinction can be drawn between policies and executive decisions. The executive decisions are the choices of action made by the local authority in each action cycle. Policies are designed precisely to give direction, consistency and regularity to these choices and the choices themselves give effect to the policies laid down.[21] In terms of the action cycle the operational policies of the authority, like its information system, exist as a loop off the main cycle, connecting with it principally between the recognition of an issue for response and the choice of action. It represents a store of possible actions from which the chosen action for a particular situation can be selected (see Fig. 3.2). Such chosen actions can change the original situation in the environment and thereby complete one action cycle.

PART TWO

The Expression of Policy

CHAPTER 4

The Nature of Policy

THE role of policy as a generic viewpoint for dealing with particular classes of situation arising in the environment has implications for the mode of its expression. For if policy has no justification other than in being brought to bear on the choice of executive actions, then its expression must perforce be related to the needs of executive decision making. On the other hand, policy is also an expression of political objectives for the actions it guides are intended to be purposive. The expression of policy therefore lies somewhere between the generalities of political objectives and the particularities of individual decisions and actions.

OBJECTIVES AND NORMS

Objectives and goals in urban planning are expressions of value in the form of statements of desired circumstances, conditions or states in the environment to which action is being directed. They may be more or less generalised. "To increase recreational opportunities", "To provide more parks", "To increase the number of tennis courts" are examples of objectives of increasing specificity. The term goal is sometimes reserved for the more general expressions, the term objective for the more specific. But both carry with them the implication of a circumstance—of increased recreational opportunities, greater park provision or more tennis courts—that is attainable once for all, although some difficulty might be found in the purely definitional task of determining what represents attainment of the more generalised goals. They all represent targets to be strived for. As such goals and objectives are not a useful form in which to express policy.

The local authority, in responding to environmental situations and controlling environmental change, is seeking to impose on the processes of change some pattern more desirable or less undesirable than it would otherwise take. It needs from its operational policies criteria by which to judge the desirable and the undesirable. An objective by its generality is not well suited to this task since it is difficult to connect specific decisions and action to general objectives. The connection exists in that there are certain relations in the activity and resource systems which the local authority is seeking to control which are conducive to the attainment of objectives. These are relations of various kinds between sets of two or more variables in the systems. Such relations are exemplified by standards which are commonly used as an expression of policy: for example, density standards relating activities to site areas, emission standards relating undesirable industrial wastes to total air or water emissions, traffic capacity standards relating vehicles to road space, housing standards relating dwelling size and facilities to household types. The assumption in each of these cases is that the attainment and maintenance of standards such as these will be contributory to the achievement of objectives—of reduced congestion, improved air and water quality, smoother traffic flow, greater housing satisfaction.

Such standards are archetypal expressions of policy.[1] The local authority can exercise its control over environmental change by applying such expressions of desirable relations between variables in the systems to situations arising in the environment to which it seeks to respond. These desired relationships include the kind of simple, two variable density, emission, traffic and accommodation standards already cited. But they also include more complex, multivariate relations. All these relationships can be regarded as norms which give expression to policy and by which executive decisions on the control of the environment are guided.

By the application of such policy norms in its control of environmental change, the local authority is using its powers to maintain through time a number of relations both between activities themselves and between these activities and land resources. The policy norms give expression to what it feels those relations should be. These relations are within the community external to the authority. At the same time the authority needs to ensure its continued operation as a controller and to this end it must maintain certain relations internal to itself to ensure that the powers, finance and manpower it needs are available; in addition the elected authority needs to sustain its continued electoral support. These are internal relations and there will be policy norms for these as well. The maintenance of these internal relations is a constraint on the effective maintenance of the external relations.[2] The local authority must therefore have policy norms for both kinds of relation.*

COMPLEMENTS, THRESHOLDS AND TRADE OFFS

While the simple, two variable standard represents the archetypal policy norm, it is by no means the only kind of norm for the expression of policy.[3] Other kinds of norm are necessary to handle the more complex, multivariate relations which planning policy dealing with complex environmental situations must seek to express. Policy norms give expression to three basic classes of relationship: complements and their converse incompatibilities, thresholds and trade offs.

Complements express essential relations between variables in the systems. Examples are requirements that buildings must be ventilated, that developments must have access to them, that all households should have homes, that capital borrowed must be repaid. Many of these relations may be so self-evident and accepted that they are hardly regarded as policy norms. The converse of complements are *incompatibilities*: for example, that there should be no frontage access to motorways, no waste discharge into rivers, no development in green belts, no industrial uses in residential areas. In either positive or negative form the relation is an absolute one. The related variables either must or must not be present at predetermined, commensurate levels of availability or provision.

Thresholds are a variation on this in which an upper or lower threshold, or both, are defined. Levels of provision or availability of variables above or below or between the thresholds, whichever is appropriate, are regarded as acceptable. Thus density standards commonly indicate maximal relations of activities to site areas, parking standards relate maximal or minimal parking provision to kinds of land use and the traffic they generate, minimal open space requirements are related to population or area, noise limits relate maximum noise to the kinds of source and the kind of recipient environment, design requirements for new developments may include an indication of those building forms or materials considered suitable. The effect of thresholds is to define a range of acceptable relations between

* See Chapter 2.

variables. As such it is a far less restrictive class of policy norm than the complement or incompatibility.

Trade offs apply where both absolute and range classes of policy norm are too confining. A trade off defines the acceptable exchange rate between the levels of one variable and another to indicate the amount of the one that may be forfeited for extra units of another. Examples would be a declared willingness to permit new development in a conservation area if it were of high architectural quality, a readiness to use land assembly powers to assist redevelopment to accommodate an expansion of town centre activities, an intention to seek such reductions of industrial emissions as are commensurate with continued operating efficiency and full employment. In all these examples there is a declared willingness to accept what may be undesirable in principle—demolition in conservation areas, land assembly costs, industrial emissions—for the sake of other desirables. Basic to such intentions is some view on how much of one is worth trading for an increment of the other. It is this view which represents the acceptable trade off.

Complements and incompatibilities, thresholds and trade offs are not entirely distinct classes of policy norm. They clearly represent a continuum from the complement case in which absolutely all or nothing is acceptable, through the thresholds which define ranges of acceptable relations, to the trade off in which the precise acceptable relations cannot be defined in advance, rather the exchange rate between the variables is defined. There are three further considerations which provide more complex variations on the nature of policy.

Firstly, much planning policy will need to be expressed in terms which will combine two or more of these classes of norm. The existence of both upper and lower thresholds is one degree of added complexity in this direction. But trade offs may be associated with thresholds. For example, there would not likely be a commitment to considering making unlimited funds available for land assembly to be undertaken for an unlimited expansion of the town centre. The authority might declare their readiness to assist in this way individual development schemes in the town centre above a minimum size and sufficient schemes to expand the town centre accommodation up to a predetermined overall maximum size. Thereby upper and lower thresholds would have been defined to identify a range in which the trade off would apply. In these ways different classes of policy norm become combined in giving expression to certain policies. In these combinations thresholds have a particular significance in defining the boundaries between one expression of policy and another.

Secondly, the desirable relation between the variables which the policy norm expresses may be linear or non-linear. A linear relationship means that with increases in one variable the desirable value of the other variable will increase or decrease in fixed proportion, so that, for example, doubling the size of an office development will double the parking requirements, or halving the storey height of the new building in the conservation area means that it needs only half the architectural quality. Such a linear relationship may not always be a true expression of policy intentions. The larger office building may be likely to accommodate activities which have a different pattern of traffic generation so that a lower unit provision of parking space may be adequate. The six-storey building may be quite as intrusive as the twelve-storey building and require just as much architectural quality to mitigate its bulk. In these ways both thresholds and trade offs may in practice be non-linear and policy norms will need to express that non-linearity.

Thirdly and most importantly, these policy relations will normally embrace more than two variables. It will almost always be a simplification to express relationships in two variable terms. Thus the simple case of the parking standard may relate parking required not just to activities but also to location; in the conservation area the trade off may not just be between the scale of the development and its architectural quality but also the activities be accommodated within it and their benefit to the town as a whole, and the opportunity provided by development to improve traffic circulation in the area.

This multivariate character of the relations for which policy norms are fixed is the essential justification for comprehensive policy in planning. Comprehensiveness in policy seeks to ensure that decisions and actions in response to different classes of situation reinforce rather than contradict each other. It recognises that it is difficult to take decisions on one situation without at the same time considering other situations arising for decision. Pressure is thereby created for all these fields of policy for different classes of situation to be brought together in a single wider field of choice.[4]

There are three basic reasons why multivariate relations necessitate comprehensive policy:

(i) The variables themselves frequently interact functionally in the workings of the activity and resource systems such that the determination of a norm to relate two or more of them necessitates policy determinations for wider variables in order to maintain those systems in functioning order. For example, parking provision and highway capacity or housing provision and employment growth are functionally related. The internal relations of the local authority are notably of this kind, since its commitment to specific programmes and policies must be demonstrably supported by its available manpower and finances.

(ii) The norms relating variables may be directed to the same goals or objectives and thereby mutually supportive. Thus land use and transportation policies may be both concerned in part at least to achieve improvements in accessibility. To leave such decisions unrelated would run the risk of achievement with one class of situation being diminished by the result of a lack of related decisions in another class of situation and an overall loss of potential effectiveness. A variation on this rationale is where the policies may relate to one area or population group. The consequence of unrelated decisions here is identical to that above except that the effectiveness is restricted to an area or population group.

(iii) The policies may also involve competition for resources. To use land or capital or manpower for one purpose means forgoing its use to satisfy other demands. It may then be necessary or desirable to extend policy to embrace restraint or alternative satisfaction of those other demands. Thus this provides the rationale for comprehensive land use allocation and comprehensive capital allocation as elements of any set of policies so that, for example, residential and industrial land availability is kept in balance, housing redevelopment and improvement are kept in step and highway and public transport policies are well related.

It is these complex patterns of relations within the subsystems of the environment which the executive decisions of the local authority seek to maintain through time: maintaining the best balance between what is desirable and what is undesirable, preventing the transgression of thresholds, securing the presence of essential complements and the absence of incompatibilities. These norms are the operational policies of the local authority acting as a basis for their choice of executive decisions.

POLICY LANGUAGES

These policy norms by which executive decisions are guided need expression in a form which will make them both intelligible and relevant to executive decision making. There is little value in a policy expressed in a manner that cannot be related to the situation with which executive action is dealing. The way in which policies are expressed will be important to the efficiency with which they can be held in and retrieved from the store of operational policies on which the authority must draw in selecting an action in response to a situation it faces and wishes in some way to control.* In particular it needs to identify the policy by characteristic attributes of the situations to which they are relevant and it needs to understand what action the policy indicates. The available languages for the expression of policy are verbal, mathematical and iconic.

The *verbal* language of words and syntax is the language in which most policy is expressed. Among the examples of policy norms above, most could be expressed in words. An example might be—

> Within the conservation area permission will not be granted for the demolition and redevelopment of those buildings listed (on the attached schedule) as buildings of individual architectural worth. Permission may, however, be granted for the demolition and redevelopment of buildings not listed there, where such redevelopment has a building use, layout and form which does not detract from the attractiveness of remaining buildings which can be viewed together with it as a group and which will enhance the conservation area as a whole through sustaining the growth of viable activities, easing the circulation of pedestrian and vehicular traffic, minimising noise or air pollution or otherwise improving environmental quality.

The *mathematical* language of symbols and equations could likewise give expression to many of the illustrative policy norms. Many of them would be simple numerical statements of thresholds typified by a parking standard for office development—

$$\text{required parking spaces} = \frac{\text{total floor space}}{1000}$$

This might be a maximum or a minimum. But equally, numerical expressions of policy norms can extend to more complex ratios and formulas. Thus the scale of the office development could enter by adding a scale factor (a)

* See Chapter 3.

which would diminish the parking space requirement for each successive equal increment of floor space in larger buildings. Additionally a locational factor (*b*) could be added which would require additional parking space in developments more distant from city centres. So that the standard might then be expressed as—

$$\text{required parking spaces} = \frac{b\,(\text{total floor space})^a}{1000}$$

In such ways this particular policy norm has taken the nature of a formula rather than a simple ratio.

The expression of policy through *iconic* language is most evidently illustrated by the conventional use of maps to express land-use allocations or proposals for transport or utility networks. Any spatially related policy can be defined on a map in this way. Graphs can give visual expression to the relationship between two variables in a two-dimensional graph or three variables in a three-dimensional graph. Other kinds of diagram, including pie graphs, networks, algorithms and bar charts, can also express policy norms.

In some circumstances words, numbers and illustrations provide alternative ways of expressing the same policy norm. A policy for a residential density gradient might be expressed in many of these ways, as in Fig. 4.1. Clearly each of these representations of the policy differs in its precision and comprehensibility. And it does so in relation both to the variables themselves, in this case resident persons, locations and site areas, and to the relationship between them. "Resident persons" needs qualification of what "resident" means even if "persons" can be hardly misinterpreted; "site areas" needs qualification through clarification of the means to be used to define and measure the site for the purpose of the density calculation. For each of these, words are the most useful medium of expression for a number of reasons. Firstly, the verbal language of words and syntax is the most varied and rich of the languages for expressing the variety of the variables with which policy is concerned; for more precise qualification of those variables, numbers or illustrations may usefully supplement words, as in defining locations. Secondly, words are the most widely understood medium of expression and in particular are the most likely medium for most of the messages coming from the community to the local authority and from the authority to the community.

But in contrast the expression of the relationship between persons and

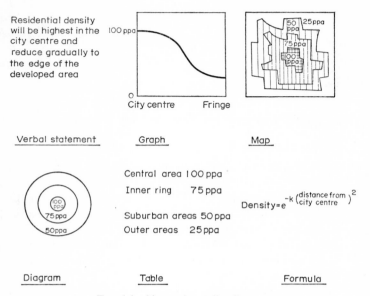

Residential density will be highest in the city centre and reduce gradually to the edge of the developed area

100 ppa

City centre   Fringe

Verbal statement   Graph   Map

Central area 100 ppa

Inner ring   75 ppa

Suburban areas 50 ppa

Outer areas   25 ppa

$$\text{Density} = e^{-k\left(\frac{\text{distance from}}{\text{city centre}}\right)^2}$$

Diagram   Table   Formula

FIG. 4.1. Alternative policy languages.

acres illustrates the shortcomings of words. Words alone cannot give expression to that relationship beyond such generalities as "high density" and "low density". Numbers are specifically required to relate persons and acres in any operationally useful way. The most precise way in which a density gradient could be expressed would be in the formula which illustrates the lack of ambiguity, economy and manipulability of numbers. On the other hand, such an expression of the policy might not be widely understood. The graphical presentation which provides equal precision might be more comprehensible. But for immediate recognition of the applicability of the policy to particular locations, the map is probably the best expression. The limitation of the map is that it can only clearly express the gradient if it is generalised into zones in place of the continuum presented by the graph and the formula. This may be a loss of precision which is worth accepting in return for higher legibility. In any case comprehensibility and precision are the two most important, though frequently conflicting, characteristics of policy languages.

CHAPTER 5

Some Dimensions of Policy in Planning

THE general view of the nature of policy takes on some added dimensions in urban planning. This is so largely because of the characteristics of urban planning as a field of public administration, specifically the classes of issues it recognises, the kinds of change it seeks to control and the particular institutions, powers, resources, professions and ideologies which have developed to effect that control. All have had their influence on the development of policy statements in planning through the emphasis given to the particular dimensions of policy.

Three dimensions have come to have significance for the expression of planning policy. There is firstly the common necessity in planning for policy to be expressed both in relation to topics—housing policy, conservation policy, transport policy—and in relation to areas—town centres, districts, villages, towns, subregions. Secondly, there is the recognised necessity of distinguishing between strategic and tactical policy, with their differing degrees of specificity and commitment. Thirdly, there is a need to clarify the expression of time in policy, especially between a dynamic strongly time-related or a more static, time-independent approach. Each of these offers a choice of emphasis for the expression of policy in planning: areas or topics, strategies or tactics, statics or dynamics.

AREAS AND TOPICS

Its concern with land resources requires an areal or spatial perspective in planning policy. At the same time its concern with activity systems requires a parallel topical perspective. These two perspectives interlock so that planning is concerned, at one and the same time, with particular activity systems extending across space and with the totality of activity systems in particular areas or spaces. The areal perspective is one of the reasons why comprehensiveness is an important attribute of policy in planning.*

Topically planning policy has traditionally been organised around a standard list of policy fields. A policy field embraces a set of integrated policies for guiding decisions on issues arising in the community which appear closely linked. The policy fields most commonly associated with urban planning are population, employment, housing, industry and commerce, transportation, shopping, education, social and community services, recreation and leisure, conservation, townscape and landscape, and utility service.[1] There is little homogeneity among the topics in this list. They have come to be regarded as different policy fields in reflection of the divisions between local and central government departments and agencies, the interests of different professions, the pattern of statutory powers and accounting conventions. They do not relate very directly to the elements of the activity and resource systems underlying environmental change. Each policy field is one or more of investment sectors, activities, land uses, environmental types or directions of change. Nor do they relate well to the kind of issues which are commonly recognised as requiring planning policy and decision. For example, is shopping as a policy field concerned with any or all of the issues of choice and accessibility for shoppers, of the adequacy of shopping accommodation for retailers, of ease of delivery, of the environmental quality of town centres or of the contribution of retailing to job opportunities? And how do policies on these issues relate, for example, to transport policy, employment policy or townscape policy? Some different pattern of policy fields is needed for planning to relate more closely to the facts about the environment subsystem and the values which underlie its recognition of issues. Such an approach might recognise five main policy fields: infrastructure, function, environmental quality, location and movement, and rate of change.

The availability and adequacy of the *infrastructure* of buildings, adapted spaces, transport and utility networks is one set of issues of concern in planning. Changing activities make continuously changing demands for their accommodation and servicing to which the supply of available infrastructure of different kinds cannot always be very rapidly adjusted, given its slow replacement rate.† Buildings and spaces designed originally for one

* See Chapter 4.
† See Chapter 1.

purpose must become used for another with or without further adaptation; transport and utility systems must be adjusted to accommodate flows above their design capacities. Some prospective activity changes will be inhibited altogether by the lack of suitable infrastructure, other changes will be accelerated and reinforced by infrastructural conditions. Through such sequences of change, planning seeks to maintain relationships between activities and the infrastructure which accommodates and services them.

The activities which the infrastructure accommodates express the *function* of an area, be it a subregion, a city, a district or a whole town. Activities of production, distribution and consumption differ greatly in the kind of goods and services they handle, the kind of employment they offer and the income they provide, not least by way of rate revenue to the local authority. So that localities differing significantly in the activities they contain will differ in this broader sense of the function they fulfil. Thus a city-fringe residential area differs functionally from an inner business area or a heavy industry dominated city from a dormitory commuter village. Because of the wide-ranging consequences of the mix of activities, changes in function are issues of great concern to planning.

Infrastructure and activity changes in turn underlie changes in *environmental quality* as experienced principally by the senses of sight and sound, but also by smell, taste and touch. Changes in the visual and aural environment are common occurrences: landscape and townscape are constantly being created and re-created as the consequence of activity and infrastructure changes on different sites, noise levels rise and fall with changes in function, particularly through the intensification or reduction of activities of production and movement. Changes in the discharge of wastes from activities on to land or into air or water and the abandonment of infrastructure contribute to land dereliction, air and water pollution. Planning policy is concerned with standards of visual appearance, noise, air and water quality.

Activities, buildings and environments exist at *locations* in space and are connected by patterns of *movement* along transport networks. A distinction can be made between within-place activities and between-place activities, and between their physical expression as land use and transport systems.* But collectively the pattern of land use and transport underlies the accessibility possessed by an area, the ease with which movement between its parts

* See Chapter 1.

may be achieved. Changes in either land use dispositions or transport networks can produce changes in this accessibility. Planning is concerned with such locational and movement issues.

These policy fields are all concerned with change: the kind of change, the accommodation of change, the environment created by change, the location of change. There are other issues relating to the *rate of change*. Changes in function, infrastructure, environmental quality, location and movement can be faster or slower or, in extreme cases, non-existent. Any policy concerned with the control of change must therefore extend to the rate of change. Building conservation policies are essentially policies for slow rates of change for buildings of particular worth. But issues relating to the speed and timing of change arise equally well with functional, infrastructural, environmental and locational change. Both too rapid change and too slow change can create problems and opportunities. For example, rapid functional change may produce high levels of unemployment pending redeployment of labour; too rapid infrastructural change may produce excessive dereliction with consequential loss of rate revenue, excessive demands on the construction industry and diminution in the quality of townscape. A rapid improvement in environmental quality may be needed to change an area's image sufficiently to attract new investment; a speedy change in land uses may be desirable to seize the opportunities provided by a new transport link. In such ways determining the appropriate rates of change is a key aspect of planning policy: the conservation policy which attempts to decelerate change, even to a standstill, and the crash programme, which attempts to accelerate change, illustrate the extreme options.

This alternative fivefold framework of policy fields fragments the whole field of planning just as the more traditional framework does. Any framework which seeks to define categories will do so. It does, however, relate more closely to the elements in the activity and resource systems which lie at the heart of planning's concerns—activities, buildings, networks, environmental attributes, locations and time periods—and the broad issues with which planning has come to be concerned—the adequacy of accommodation and utilities, the quality of the environment, travel time and costs, local economic development and the conservation of valued assets. In these ways this framework of policy fields provides a more useful perspective on the topical concerns of planning policy.

Areally planning has traditionally adopted the geographical concept of a hierarchy of areas to which to relate policy.[2] This extends down from regions, through subregions, towns and districts to zones with each level of the hierarchy defined in relation to some criterion. Administrative areas rarely accord even approximately with this neat concept: subregions are divided between counties, towns are cut off from their hinterlands, ward boundaries are not related to urban spatial structures.[3] Nevertheless the administrative boundaries are significant both because they are frequently basic to data availability and because policies, decisions and actions must finally be applied to administrative units. Policy areas must be a compromise between theory and practice. Such a pragmatic approach means that no single, unambiguous criterion can determine the areas to which planning policy will relate. The definition of areas and the definition of topics must be closely related since the areas only have relevance in relation to the policy issues for which they form a convenient spatial framework. Some issues will be more amenable to analysis and policy making for larger areas; others will be more suitably dealt with at the smaller scale. On this basis a standard three-tier hierarchy of planning areas can be defined—subregions, districts and zones—while accepting that expansions or contractions of this system will in circumstances be necessary.

Subregions form the upper tier for urban planning policy. A subregion generally forms an area in which some fairly well-developed local economy is established with a significant basic sector, such as manufacturing, tourism or national administration, providing goods and services for export beyond the subregion. The subregional income provided by this basic sector will in turn support the non-basic sector producing goods and services for consumption by the local population.[4] Spatially a subregion will also tend to comprise a journey to work area in which employment and resident population are in approximate balance and across the boundaries of which there is relatively little commuting.[5] Thus functional and locational and movement issues are dominant in defining subregions. Subregions may well be characterised by their environment, infrastructure or rate of change, but these will be generally less significant as criteria.

Districts will vary greatly in size and nature. Some will be large tracts of rural land, others will be whole small towns, yet others will be areas within larger towns or cities. They are unlikely to have their own economies or to be self-contained in commuting terms, but they may be relatively self-contained in relation to social, shopping and educational activities and trips.

In this sense districts will frequently have a definable service function. Equally important may be a homogeneity of infrastructure in terms of the type, age and condition of building stock and utilities within districts, and a related homogeneity of environmental quality, in particular visual appearance and air quality. The predominant issues in defining districts are likely then to be functional issues relating to service provision, infrastructural and environmental issues. Location and movement issues and rate of change issues will not be so significant in defining districts.

Zones are the smallest unit of this standard three-tier system of areas for the expression of policy. Smaller units will be necessary for the storage and retrieval of information* and for the analytical work in policy making and review.† Zones will be even more diverse than districts. They will rarely have a functional homogeneity or raise movement or locational issues which can define them. They may well have very characteristic infrastructures and environments but the defining issues for zones will normally be the rate of change to which they are subject. Thus redevelopment areas, general improvement areas, new housing areas, conservation areas are all examples of zones defined in relation to some particular rate of change.

This hierarchy of areas only establishes the most basic distinctions between different kinds of area suited to the expression of planning policy. It needs elaboration and adjustment both in relation to local circumstances of geography and administration and in relation to specific local definitions of planning issues. It illustrates, however, how interlinked are the definitions of topics on the one hand and of areas on the other as the twin perspective from which planning policy can be viewed.

STRATEGIES AND TACTICS

All executive decisions in planning are not equal in their impact. Some decisions clearly produce greater changes in activities and their call on resources than others. Some do this directly by effecting major actions, some do this indirectly by triggering significant chain reactions among activities. The majority of the change in the environment system is probably always caused by a minority of the decisions. Among executive decisions there is then a distinction which can be drawn between the greater, strategic decisions and the lesser, tactical decisions.[6]

* See Chapter 3.
† See Chapter 10.

Strategic decisions are generally reached through a wide-ranging consideration of the main alternative choices of action available, the objectives to which those alternatives are directed, and the desirability of those objectives. For such fundamental considerations the alternative actions can only be broadly specified and their consequences can only be expressed at a low level of detail so that an overview is possible. In contrast, tactical decisions are taken with the benefit of more detailed specification of the choices, but they are only considered incrementally within the context set by previous strategic decisions, without wide considerations of alternatives and their relationship to objectives. The two kinds of decision making neutralise each other's shortcomings: incremental tactical decision making helps to overcome the relative unreality of strategic decisions and fundamental strategic decision making helps to right the conservative bias of tactical incrementalism. Chess playing provides a valuable analogy: the player cannot afford the time to reassess all possible moves at every turn; instead he selects a strategy, increments tactically within that strategy for a few moves, then reappraises the strategic situation either because of danger signs which can be observed some moves ahead or because he wishes to explore whether the ever-changing situation allows an even better strategy.[7]

Scale of effect is the most evident criterion for identifying a strategic decision. Any change which involves an increase or decrease in some environmental variable which is great relative to its existing state will be a fundamental change. In this it is not the absolute but the marginal scale of change which matters. Each policy field can provide examples of individual decisions or actions with major impacts—industrial closures and the consequent loss of employment, large development schemes with extensive land-use changes, new industrial processes producing significantly reduced atmospheric emissions over a wide area, new buildings which by virtue of their siting or their bulk have a widespread visual impact. In each of these cases what is essentially a single decision has a major environmental impact.

But changes which by themselves have minor effects in scale terms may nevertheless be so highly interactive that they initiate a succession of other changes which cumulatively represent a major effect. Examples might be an improved link in a transport network which restructures travel patterns across a wide area, the removal of an individual building which is a significant element in a townscape, the demolition of particular housing accommodation which acted as an essential link in a housing filter. Thus scale of effect and interaction of effect are the two indicators of strategic decisions in planning.

If a distinction between strategic and tactical decisions is recognised, then a distinction between strategic and tactical policy must be drawn. Strategic decisions can only be guided by strategic policy, tactical decisions by tactical policy. This necessity is the implication of the law of requisite variety in cybernetics: "only variety can destroy variety".[8] A system of given variety, by which is meant the number of distinct elements in the system or the number of states of the system, can only be controlled by a controlling system of comparable variety. So that changes specified and detailed at a certain level of resolution cannot be related to policies expressed at considerably higher or lower levels of detail: for example, the decision to release a large tract of land for new residential development cannot be determined by the policies which are relevant to the decision to grant permission for an individual house on a site within that area—the former raises broader considerations than the latter and must be related to more broadly expressed policy.

Because strategic decisions have major impacts, either directly or indirectly, strategic policy is more long term. The more major the decision the greater the share of total resources, particularly of land and capital, thereby committed and the longer the system must live with the commitment. Major commitments such as new sewerage works, a smoke-control zone, a housing-improvement area or new employment opportunities can only be accepted on one of two grounds. Either they can be accepted as part of a comprehensive policy which will secure well into the future necessary supportive decisions and actions—for example, residential land allocations for the sewerage works, restrictions on industrial emissions for the smoke-control zone, restrictions on housing redevelopment for the housing improvement area, new transport connections for the new employment. Or alternately where these kinds of related decisions cannot be guaranteed, major commitments can be accepted upon demonstration that they are robust enough to withstand the uncertainties of the future or flexible enough to be capable of adaptation through subsequent tactical decisions. In one or other of these ways, through being comprehensive or being demonstrably robust or flexible, strategic policy can take a form which suits it to its necessarily long term nature. It will also, particularly where it is comprehensive, need to be more corporate in its making.

Tactical policy will in contrast be shorter term, less comprehensive, less necessarily robust or flexible and can be less corporate in its making. It is shorter term because of its focus on the minor decisions with their lesser commitments of resources and lesser need for supportive decisions or actions or demonstrable flexibility or robustness. Tactical policy will also tend to be concerned not with the comprehensive whole, but with one topic or one area at a time. Topically based tactical policy might be concerned with function and the local economy as a policy field; areally based tactical policy might be concerned with one district or one zone. In either case they will take policy for other topics or other areas as given.

Strategic policy's expression of the totality of policies, both from areal and topical perspectives, can only be at a lower level of detail than tactical policy's expression of partial policy. Strategic policy in urban planning will tend to be concerned with movement corridors, tactical policy with specific road alignments; strategic policy with the distribution of activities between zones, tactical policy with land uses on specific sites; strategic policy with changes which will accrue over quinquennia, tactical policy with change accruing annually. This distinction in specificity between strategy and tactics extends beyond the definition of policy variables to the nature of the relations between them and the choice of policy language. Complements and incompatibilities are more likely to be found as policy norms in tactical policy and trade offs as policy norms in strategic policy; thresholds may be found in both. Simply because it is so wide-ranging, longer term, generalised and subject to uncertainty the less restrictive kinds of policy norm are most appropriate to strategic policy and, conversely, the more confining kinds of norm are suited to the narrower, shorter term, more detailed, less uncertain tactical policy. Equally the more precise iconic language of maps and mathematical language of numbers and formulae will be the appropriate media for expressing tactical policy, the richer but less precise verbal language of words and diagrams will be appropriate for strategic policy.

There can be no absolute distinction between strategic and tactical policy.[9] Higher level decisions will always be strategic in relation to lower-level decisions, and decisions that appear strategic in one circumstance may appear tactical in another. The distinction is relative rather than absolute. Nevertheless it is a distinction of great significance for both the expression and making of policy in planning.

STATICS AND DYNAMICS

Policy in planning is commonly focused on the medium and the long-term future. But policy is intended to serve as a guide in making the executive decisions of the present and immediate future. Policy making cannot be a once for all exercise in decision making for the next 10, 15 or 20 years, determining now all the decisions likely to be needed in that period in order to get consistency between them. Rather it is an attempt to bring into joint consideration classes of issue on which decisions will be needed. Some of these issues may arise immediately; but it is more likely, since the inter-action between the community and its government is continuous, that while some may be arising immediately, others may be expected shortly and yet others may only be foreseen in an indeterminate future. The time dimension is therefore an inescapable dimension of policy.

Of all the fields of public administration planning has probably tradition-ally sought to make policy for the longest time periods. Whereas in other fields 10 years may be regarded as long term and a limit on the period to which consideration should be given, planning commonly views such a period as medium term. Planning's time periods are broadly 0–5 years as short term, 5–15 years as medium term, 15–25 years as long term. This longer policy time scale in urban planning derives largely from character-istics of the processes of change which planning seeks to control:

(i) Urban development projects have long lead times for their prepara-tion and implementation—rarely less than 2 years and anything up to 10 years for highway construction, town-centre development, extensive use changes. The reasons for these long lead times are frequently institutional: the fragmentation of land ownership, the complexity of legal and statutory procedures for purchase of land and authorisation of development, the dependence of development on the availability of capital and the necessity of design work unique to each development.*

(ii) Land resources are not easily substituted, particularly where they have unique topographical or locational characteristics; nor is land developed for one use easily transferred to another use. This gives rise to a need in planning to safeguard sites for future allocation to

* See Chapter 2.

particular activities with specific site requirements or locational requirements, especially important where the extension of networks or established land uses is under consideration.

(iii) Urban infrastructure has a long life:* in broad terms housing lasts up to 100 years, industrial buildings up to 80 years, central areas 50–80 years, roads in their location 100 or more years and in their construction possibly 30 years. While the capital value of the infrastructure may be written off in purely financial terms over shorter periods, there remains a desire to maximise its utility by ensuring a continuing compatibility between structures, uses and locations.

(iv) Much urban change is slow and substantially changed conditions can consequently only be brought about over long periods of time. The longer-term benefits may be so considerable as to justify their consideration in policy making in some way.† Moreover, it may only be in the long term that the total effect of some policy, particularly in such physical terms as a completed highway network or a rebuilt town centre, will be apparent and some presentation of that totality may be desirable as a component of policy.

Within the 0–25 year time frame, planning policy may treat time statically or dynamically. If statically, the policy norms will express states of the environmental system at one or more points in time. They will take a form which could be described as end states, blueprints or snapshots. They will tend to indicate the aggregate relations between variables in the system which should prevail at those points in time. These might be expressed, for example, in tables showing how many jobs of what kind there will be, maps showing which land will be used for what purpose and the overall pattern of the transport network, verbal accounts of the environmental character each area should have, diagrams showing the pattern of traffic-free areas to be created in a town centre.

If policy treats time dynamically, the policy norms will tend to express more disaggregate relations between variables in the system to be maintained over time, including progressively changing relations if necessary. These might be expressed as ratios of male:female, blue collar:white collar, basic:non-basic employment to be sought in major employment growth or decline, diagrams showing the dependence of subsequent transport network

* See Chapter 1.
† See Chapter 10.

extensions or land-use allocations on the outcome of earlier ones, verbal statements of acceptable and unacceptable changes in environmental character, graphs showing annual or quinquennial rates of new additions to the housing stock, curves showing relations between pedestrian safety and amenity and vehicular accessibility which will guide street closures in a town centre. In these ways, and in contrast to static statements, the dynamic forms of policy norm are much more statements of directions, processes and rates of change.

This dynamic approach may itself take one of two forms dependent on the degree to which it seeks to indicate the points in time at which issues will emerge for decision and action. On the one hand, the likely timing and sequence of decision points, as well as the policy norms to be applied, could be specified in the policy. This has been called Cook's Tour planning in analogy with the prearranged itinerary. In practice minor changes can still be accommodated *en route* with this kind of policy statement so that this approach then becomes a kind of contingency planning. On the other hand, policy may only specify a general direction of movement, possibly indicating some of the earlier decision points, but putting more emphasis on the norms to be applied as and when issues for decision arise. This has been called Lewis and Clark planning in analogy with pioneer exploration.[10]

These static and dynamic expressions of policy are clearly related since the end states are integrals of the changes—the outcome of the acceptable environmental changes will be the desired total environmental character, maintenance of the housing redevelopment, improvement and new construction rates will achieve the specified age and condition structure of the housing stock, applications of the trade-off curve should result in the pattern of pedestrian areas specified. But the distinction between ways of handling time are not purely academic. For the approaches differ in the ease and confidence with which policy can be expressed in one form or another, the comprehensibility they give to policy and their relevance to the needs of executive decision making. These will all differ between circumstances so that policy in urban planning will sometimes need to take one or other of these forms: sometimes emphasising an end state, sometimes emphasising the processes of change, sometimes expressing a determinate view of these processes, sometimes an indeterminate view.

Static expressions of end states will have great illustrative value. The maps, verbal descriptions and tabulations of a fixed end state will probably have greater immediacy and comprehensibility as an expression of policy intention than the more disaggregate expressions of change processes. They present a picture of the future which can be contrasted directly with the known picture of the present to indicate in fairly precise form where the changes are coming. The blueprint is in this way a relatively simple way of marshalling together multifarious strands of policy to view them and present them as a coherent whole. In certain circumstances, where time perspectives are shorter term, where great certainty exists about the issues which will arise, the blueprint may also be a suitable guide to executive decision making. In such circumstances each individual decision may be completing a recognisable part of the whole picture. This will likely be true of some detailed, narrow, tactical policy. But otherwise when the gap between the present and the blueprint is too great to make it possible to relate the individual issue to it, then the blueprint will have limited value for guiding executive decisions. In these circumstances too it will be difficult to draw up a blueprint with confidence. A longer time scale, a broader range of topics or areas, a lesser detail will all compound uncertainties to diminish confidence in the making of blueprints.

In these circumstances the more disaggregate expressions of dynamic policy will probably be easier to achieve. And at the same time they may provide a more directly applicable guide to executive decision making. The more specific time frame of Cook's Tour planning will provide a closer guide than the Lewis and Clark approach, but may be harder to achieve. The dynamic statements may provide a less integrating device than the blueprint, but it may be all that is possible. It will, however, be weaker than the blueprint in its comprehensibility.

ACTION CYCLES REFORMULATED

Planning policies have been characterised as generic viewpoints for dealing with recurrent classes of issue calling for decision.* These policies are expressed as relations between activities in all their variety and between those activities and land resources. And these relations may take the form of complements, incompatibilities, thresholds or trade offs and be expressed verbally, mathematically or iconically. This is the view of the nature and role of policy in the simple action cycle model. The local authority, in seeking

* See Chapter 4.

possible responses to situations arising in the community which it has recognised as issues calling for action, can refer to its store of policies and use the relations expressed there as norms against which to assess the changes which its response might allow or encourage. Would minimum thresholds be met and maximum thresholds not be transgressed? Would complements be assured and incompatibilities be avoided? Would appropriate rates of trade off be achieved.

These sets of norms which express operational policies need to be additionally structured along these further dimensions as topical or areal relations, as strategic or tactical relations, as static or dynamic relations. Thus the complements might relate to areas or topics; or the thresholds might be strategic or tactical; or the trade offs might be static or dynamic or any other combination of these different dimensions of policy.

A proposal to establish a major new government office centre in a medium sized town centre might come to the local authority. Of such a proposal it might be asked—will the change in employment, both directly and indirectly through multiplier effects, accord with strategically desired changes in employment structure or tactically reduce local unemployment? Locationally is the proposed development compatible with the immediate capacity of the transport system and does it accord in the longer term with the land-use pattern envisaged by relating to the location of new residential districts and thereby enhancing the possibility of maintaining public transport connections? Are the quantity and quality of accommodation and ancillary provision, for example parking, up to minimum standards? Environmentally does the proposal provide a reasonable case for an enlarged scale of building development which policy envisages only in exceptional cases in the town centre? Can all the interacting elements respond without excessive malfunction—avoiding excess labour demand, traffic congestion or housing shortage especially—to this rapid rate of change in new employment? In these questions there are elements of all the aspects of policy: of complements (transport capacity), thresholds (parking) and trade offs (building scale); of areas (town centre) and topics (location and movement); of strategy (employment structure) and tactics (unemployment rate); of statics (land-use pattern) and dynamics (housing availability). Policy statements, if they are to adequately serve executive decision making in urban planning, must be able to express such a variety of relations.

CHAPTER 6

Policy Statements

A LARGE variety of policy statements have come into use in planning in response to the need for means of giving expression to urban environmental policy in all its diversity. Some, notably the local authority development plan, have been created by statute, others have developed through usage and convention; some are directed principally at the expression of planning policy, others serve as policy statements incidentally to their main purpose which may be concerned with the internal management of local or central government financial and other resources.

Thus there are county maps, town maps and comprehensive area maps, transportation studies, subregional studies, traffic and transport plans, town centre maps, village plans, capital investment programmes, conservation areas, general improvement areas, smoke control areas, structure plans, Regulation 8 plans, district plans, action area plans and subject plans as well as the general device of stating local authority policy by means of formally adopted resolutions in council minutes. Some of these can state policy comprehensively, some can state policy only for one topic, some are more geared to strategic, some more to tactical policy, some are focused on large areas, some on small, some offer scope for dynamic expressions of policy, some only for static expressions. But most significantly, some are only now emergent, the products of recent statute or experience, while others are passing into disuse. In the future, planning policy seems likely to be given expression principally through three kinds of policy statement—structure plans, programmes and local plans—each with something particular to contribute in expressing the diversity of policy needs.

1962 ACT DEVELOPMENT PLANS[1]

Under the Town and Country Planning Act, 1962,[2] which largely restated the development plan provisions of the Town and Country Planning

Act 1947, the general purpose of a development plan is to indicate the manner in which the local planning authority propose that land in the area of the plan should be used and the stages by which any development proposed should be carried out. To achieve this purpose a plan may in particular define the sites of proposed roads, buildings and open spaces, allocate land for agricultural, industrial or other use, and designate land as subject to compulsory purchase. The form and content of plans vary between county councils and county borough councils. The county development plan consists of[3]

(i) a county map and written statement for all of an authority's area;
(ii) town maps and written statements for urban areas within the county;
(iii) comprehensive development area maps and written statements for areas within the county.

In addition, there is the report of survey including the written analysis which sets out the circumstances of the area, its problems and opportunities; while not legally part of the development plan, this is required to be submitted in support of it. Other kinds of documents—notably supplementary town maps, compulsory purchase designation maps, town and comprehensive development area programme maps—were originally part of the 1962 Act development plan, but were later no longer required. Programming was then to be indicated instead in the written statement. The form and content of county borough development plans are the same except that there is no county map; the town map and written statement, covering the whole of the authority's area, is in these cases the premier document. All these component parts of the development plan were to be exposed to the local public before being submitted to the Minister of Housing and Local Government (now the Secretary of State for the Environment). The Minister issued a decision on the plan after holding a public inquiry into objections.

The *county map and written statement* covers the whole of an administrative county. The map, on an Ordnance Survey base at a scale of 1 inch to 1 mile, shows by symbols settlements intended as centres for social, educational or welfare services, as well as main roads and areas defined for mineral working, national defense, government or local authority departments, green belts, areas of landscape, historic or scientific value and other proposals of importance. It does not differentiate between what exists and what is proposed. It also indicates areas to be covered by town maps or comprehensive development area maps or to be designated as the sites of new towns. The written statement is a very short formal document containing a verbal summary of the main policies and proposals of the plan and their programming. A report of survey, comprising maps, diagrams and a written analysis indicating the basis of the plan, accompanies this while not formally part of the development plan.[4]

The *town map and written statement* is for county boroughs and urban areas within administrative counties. At a larger Ordnance Survey scale of 6 inch to 1 mile, it shows essentially zones for primary land uses together with densities for the whole of the area covered. Like county maps, town maps also define sites for specific uses like minerals, airfields, green belts and so on, as well as main roads, but again no distinction is made between existing and proposed development. Areas included in a comprehensive development area map are also indicated. The written statement again summarises verbally including programming and a report of survey substantiates the proposals.

The *comprehensive development area map and written statement* is for areas which should be developed or redeveloped as a whole. The Ordnance Survey scale at 1:2500 is yet larger, but the map again defines sites for specific uses, including roads, allocates other zones for more general uses and also designates land for compulsory purchase. Again the written statement provides a verbal summary and programme and the report of survey a substantiation.

These three levels of policy statement in the 1962 Act development plan are distinguished principally by the degree of detail with which essentially comparable kinds of policy are presented. From the county plan through to the comprehensive development area plan the scale of map and the precision of use category increase so that proposed developments coming up for executive decision could be more exactly related to the provisions of the plan. But this is almost the only significant distinction between the levels.

OTHER POLICY STATEMENTS

Apart from these components of the development plan, local authorities have found it necessary to prepare various other kinds of environmental policy statements. These have largely developed to express policy in relation to particular kinds of executive decisions to which the development plan could not very adequately relate, either because of the development plan's relatively narrow emphasis on land use or the lengthiness of planmaking, review and approval procedures.[5] At the same time, the management of both central and local government financial resources has become increasingly geared to policy objectives and a number of policy statements have come into use as prerequisites to investment decisions by government. Among this class of policy statements other than development plans are policy resolutions, informal plans, investment programmes and area designations.

Of these, *policy resolutions* for particular topics are probably more common in urban planning than any of the others. To make a statement of policy a local authority, in the normal way of things, only needs to make a resolution which becomes recorded in the council minutes. This applies to planning as much as to other fields of administration and most local authorities supplement their development plans with policy resolutions of this kind, in particular where circumstances necessitate the clarification of policy on some individual aspect of planning in order that executive decisions on that aspect can be made. Such statements might relate to particular activities or land uses or kinds of development either generally or in particular parts of their area, for example policy on mineral exploitation in a county or facing materials for new buildings in a historic town.

Of the informal plans which have come into use the most widespread are subregional studies, transportation studies, traffic and transport plans, town centre maps and village plans. *Subregional studies* have been prepared by neighbouring local authorities in subregions. The intention is that they should serve as a bridge between regional considerations and the development plans of local authorities by providing the authorities concerned with a subregional framework of agreed policy for their individual policy statements. To this end the studies are concerned in particular to explore alternative policies for accommodating population growth over the next 20–30 years in terms of housing, employment, shopping, transport and recreation, while paying regard to the potential of existing towns, the linkages between parts of subregions and the resources of the countryside.[6] Their outputs are generally written policy statements on the function of the subregion, expressed in future population and employment levels and structures, locational policies for additional residential, employment and sometimes retailing provision as well as inter-urban road proposals, and less frequently policy for housing and utilities, infrastructure and landscape conservation. The intention has been to concentrate on issues needing resolution at the subregional scale.

Transportation studies were initiated first in the conurbations and later in medium-sized towns and cities. They are intended to provide a policy statement against which projects can be brought forward for inclusion in national transport investment programmes and by which the operation of existing transport systems, for example, through traffic and public transport management, can be guided.[7] The transportation study is directed to developing transport policies covering public transport, the road network and parking policies devised to match a complementary land-use pattern. Their policy output is in future to be expressed in *Transport Policies and Programmes* for each county, with sections for each main urban area. They will cover transport policies for 10–15 years ahead, together with 5-year expenditure programmes rolled forward annually. They will provide a basis for decisions on government grants and loan sanctions. Preparation of Transport Policies and Programmes has to be integrated as far as possible with work on the development plan and where considerations are common to both they should rest on common or related studies.[8] *Traffic and transport plans* were introduced as additional means of expressing in a coordinated way short term policies for the management of traffic, the operation of public transport and the control of parking to secure both transport and environmental objectives.[9] They cover these policies for the next seven years or so.

Town centre maps have been used to express policies for redevelopment, improvement and conservation of town centres which go beyond the statements of roads and use zones which could be shown in a comprehensive development area map.[10] Their concern is essentially with the functions, layout and environment of town centres, and with integrating the processes of land assembly, public works and private development by which change in these could be secured. The form of policy statement is diagrammatic, showing areas in which particular policies, for example, for conservation or the elimination of through traffic, could be pursued as well as land uses and transport proposals of varying degrees of commitment. The main diagram is normally supplemented and cross referenced by supporting explanatory or illustrative reports, maps and diagrams. *Village plans* and plans for small towns are similar to town centre plans as policy statements and, like them, are to be shaped in form and content to local circumstances.[11] They are intended to indicate sites required by public authorities for schools, roads, community centres and other uses, sites for private developments and policies or standards applying to all or part of the area. The form of policy statement is normally a written statement of principles with or without illustration on a map, and supplementary layouts and design schemes.

Capital investment programmes are an increasingly common expression of local authorities' internal management. In these are set out, frequently sector by sector, the capital investment for land acquisition and new building and the related costs of staffing and running the buildings and the services they provide on a year by year basis. Sometimes the emphasis is on capital works, sometimes on capital and recurrent expenditure. Principally such programmes are intended to both secure that the development of the authority's service is possible with the resources, chiefly of land and capital, likely to be available and to provide a means of programming related developments. The requirements of central government for either the regular submission of projects for incorporation in national rolling programmes or for the occasional submission of plans for the development of one service or another have frequently been instrumental in the development of investment programmes. The form of policy statement provided by investment programmes is commonly a schedule of projects, detailed with regard to content, timing and interrelationships and a statement of the associated capital and recurrent expenditure. They usually cover local authority's own expenditure only, although links with committed private actions and investments may be identified.

Lastly, besides policy resolutions, informal plans and investment programmes, statutory provisions exist for the designation of areas in which particular kinds of policy will be pursued: these are areas of special advertisement control, smoke-control areas, conservation areas, and general improvement areas. *Areas of special control* may be designated in which particularly stringent control over the display of advertisements takes effect.[12] *Smoke control areas* are areas in which restrictions on domestic fuel and industrial emissions may be imposed and in which payments may be made towards the cost of converting burners to smokeless fuel.[13] Both these kinds of designated area require the approval of the Secretary of State for the Environment.

Conservation areas are areas of special architectural or historic interest, the character or appearance of which it is desired to protect or enhance through policies and proposals to be brought forward by the local authority and for which specific grants are available.[14] The policy statement here comprises essentially only the definition of the area on a map, but commonly supplemented by details of the particular buildings or environmental characteristics which have led to designation and the policies which are to be pursued to enhance the area. *General improvement areas* are predominantly existing residential areas in which the local authority, partly financed by central government grants, intends to secure the improvement of both houses and their environments through the payment of grants and loans to private owners, and through improvement of dwellings and environment by the authority themselves.[15] The policy statement is a definition of the area and details of the proposals for improvement to be pursued by the local authority.

1971 ACT DEVELOPMENT PLANS[16]

To this great variety of policy statements have now been added the new forms of development plan introduced by the Town and Country Planning Act, 1968, now consolidated in the Town and Country Planning Act, 1971.[17] The purpose of the 1971 Act development plan is to present policies and proposals for the development and other use of land in an area. While the focus of the plan is, like the 1962 Act development plan, upon physical development, policies and proposals are not simply to be expressed in land-use terms. A range of other considerations have been brought into the development plan—specifically an integrated approach to land-use and transportation planning, measures for improving the physical environment, the implementation of regional planning, questions of capital resource availability and allocation, and social considerations.[18] The development plan consists of

(i) the structure plan written statement and key diagram for all or part of an authority's area; the structure plan may also incorporate a supplementary Regulation 8 plan;

(ii) local plan proposals, maps and written statements for areas within the structure plan; local plans may be district plans, action area plans or subject plans.

In addition the report of survey accompanies but is not part of the plan. After April 1974, structure plans will be a responsibility of the new county authorities and local plans will be a county or district authority responsibility dependent on an agreement to be reached between them in each case.[19] Both of these component parts of the development plan must be made available for public inspection but only the structure plan must be submitted to and approved by the Secretary of State for the Environment who may hold a public examination of the policy issues dealt with in the plan.[20] After a structure plan has been approved, local plans may be adopted by resolution of the local authority itself which must have held a public inquiry into objections.

The *structure plan* will cover the whole or a substantial part of the authority's area. It consists of a written statement, the key diagram, any other diagrams, illustrations or descriptive matter explaining or illustrating the proposals in the plan, and the Secretary of State's notice of approval of the plan.[21] The written statement should cover the context of national and regional policy and local circumstances in which the plan has been prepared, the objectives of the plan and the reasoning behind and full explanation of the proposed overall strategy and its component policies and general proposals, including their relationship to each other and to the likely availability of resources. These policies can relate to population, employment, housing, industry and commerce, transportation, shopping, education, other social and community services, recreation and leisure, conservation, townscape and landscape and utility services. The key diagram supplements the written statement by showing graphically, but not on an Ordnance Survey base, policies and general proposals in the plan, and other illustrations may clarify the written statement. The written statement and diagram will both identify the location of action areas for which more detailed plans will be prepared. The report of survey should summarise the findings of surveys, the projection of trends into the future, the analysis of issues for which policy is needed and the alternative policies which have been considered and the reasons for their rejection—all this in sufficient detail to validate the decisions included in the plan. It may also include a 10-year programme indicating the progress it is hoped to make in approximately the 10-year period following submission of the plan to the Secretary of State.

Regulation 8 plans are for urban areas within counties where there are major planning issues needing consideration in a more closely argued and self-contained form than would be possible if treated only as items in a county-wide plan, even if detailed in subsequent local plans. Such areas may, with the consent of the Secretary of State, be dealt with in a supplementary part of the development plan, to be treated as a structure plan.

Local plans will cover small or large areas within the area of the local planning authority and within the period covered by the authority's structure plan. Local plans enable the expression of more detailed policy to implement or extend the policy and general proposals of the structure plan, with which they must conform. Each local plan will consist of a proposals map, a written statement, any other diagrams, illustrations and descriptive matter explaining or illustrating the proposals in the plan and the local planning authority's resolution of adoption of the plan.[22] The proposals map is prepared on an Ordnance Survey map base at any appropriate scale. It defines sites where the authority is committed to change of a specified nature, and identifies areas within which particular policies are to be pursued such as exclusion of through traffic or changes in building use. The written statement will explain the background of the plan, including the relevant provisions of the structure plan, the decisions it contains, their relationships and timing and how they were reached. A report of survey, separate from that for the structure plan, is not a requirement for local plans. These general characteristics vary somewhat between district plans, action area plans and subject plans.

District plans are comprehensive policy statements for relatively large areas in which change is expected to take place largely in piecemeal fashion and at a relatively slow and uneven pace: parts of large towns, smaller towns in counties—other than those for which Regulation 8 plans have been prepared—and rural parts of counties or individual villages. Any firm proposal, conforming generally with the structure plan, may be included whether or not it is for early executive action or will produce a major change in the area, and policies to be applied within the whole or parts of the area through the time period of the structure plan can be expressed. *Action area plans* are also comprehensive policy statements, but for areas which have been indicated in the structure plan as those in which intensive and relatively rapid change by redevelopment, development or improvement by public or private agencies seems certain to commence within 10 years of the submission of the structure plan to the Secretary of State. Action area plans might, for example, be used to secure coordination of projects between a local authority, other public agencies and private developers in developing a new housing area, redeveloping a town centre or inserting new roads and associated redevelopment in built up areas. The plan might vary from a fully worked up and costed programme for the restoration of derelict land or the renewal of a conservation area to an outline brief for a new housing area which sets out a framework of requirements and objectives within which the developer and his architects should work. *Subject plans* give detailed treatment of particular aspects or issues where policies or proposals must be formulated in advance of a comprehensive type of local plan or a comprehensive plan is not needed. Examples might be the landscaping of a motorway corridor or the recreational use of a river valley.

POLICY FRAMEWORK

All these kinds of policy statement are currently in use or in preparation. But as the nature of the issues which planning recognises and the kinds of response to those issues which it adopts change over time, so the relevance and usefulness of particular kinds of policy statement increase or decrease. Some of these currently operative policy statements are finding wider application, others are falling into disuse or becoming transmuted into or merged with others. In particular three trends are prevalent: the formal changeover from the 1962 Act to the 1971 Act development plans, the demise of many kinds of informal policy statement, and the emergence of more corporate statements of policy for local authorities as a whole.

The provisions of the Town and Country Planning Act 1971 regarding development plans did not come into effect immediately or universally. Rather they have been introduced progressively through statutory instruments called commencement orders as and when local authorities have become ready to operate them.[23] Moreover, the existing local authority development plan remains in force until a structure plan and an adequate coverage of local plans has been achieved; in the meantime any amendments to 1962 Act development plans should apply the principles of the 1971 Act as far as possible.[24] The policies in a structure or local plan will, however, prevail over those of a 1962 Act plan. Since the 1971 Act development plan has been introduced progressively in different areas, since the preparation and approval of structure plans must take time and since local plans cannot be adopted until after the approval of a structure plan, then a complete changeover to the new form of development plan will take time. It may well be towards the end of the 1970s before the new system is fully operational in all areas.

When that has been achieved the need for a number of other informal plans will disappear. Some of these, notably subregional studies, town centre maps and village plans, were introduced as means of overcoming the recognised shortcomings of the 1962 Act development plans. To a large extent the characteristics of the structure and local plans as policy statements reflect the experience gained in operating with these informal policy statements. Many plans of this kind will be superseded by up-to-date development plans. But development plans as policy statements will still have characteristics which make them unsuited to certain kinds of policy, particularly the statutory restrictions on their content and on procedures for their preparation and approval. This may be too limiting a form for certain statements of tactical policy, particularly where there is an important investment element, for which non-statutory, topically based programmes which allow speedier amendment and review will continue to be needed.

Lastly, the growth of a wider interest in policy throughout all fields of public administration in both central and local government must have its effect. In local government there has been the development of ideas of corporate policy making, frequently called corporate planning. This development has its basis in the view that a local authority's decisions and actions on the increasingly complex issues it faces should be less compartmentalised by departments and services and more expressive of political objectives.[25] In cases this movement has led to internal reorganisation of departments and committees within local authorities; in other cases it has led to revised procedures for coordinating decision making through management boards, cross membership of committees and the establishment of corporate planning teams.[26] In all cases it represents an attempt to strengthen the policy making and review function throughout the authority and to put policy on a more corporate, less departmental, sectoral or service basis. The precise form of policy statements these processes are intended to provide as output is less certain.[27] In some cases, particularly where the impetus has come from pressure upon capital and financial resources, it is

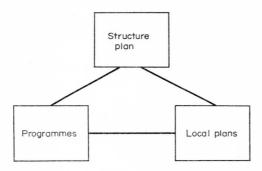

Fig. 6.1. Policy framework.

leading to a new presentation of the annual budget with the expenditure related not simply to traditionally defined services but to objectives and with expenditures and incomes projected up to 5 years ahead. In other cases, particularly where the impetus has come from reappraisals of the needs faced by the authority's services, emphasis has been on the development of medium term policy plans in which policies for the operation and development of the local authority's different services are related to their changing social, economic and environmental context. There is a further concept of a community plan which would be a statement of policy embracing all kinds of governmental control of change in the community, not simply those achieved through the provision of local authority's services and the exercise of local authority regulatory powers, but including the policies of all units of local government and policies of central government and other public authorities which have impacts on the local community.[28]

The future framework of policy statements for the expression of environmental policy will be an outcome of these trends. The three key elements in that framework are likely to be the structure plan, the topic by topic programmes and the area by area local plans standing in some kind of relationship to each other, as indicated in Fig. 6.1. The precise nature of the relationships and the separate roles for each kind of policy statement which those relationships will sustain will depend on their capacities to express the varied dimensions of planning policy: their choice of language, their topical and areal bases, their comprehensiveness, their strategic or tactical nature and their ways of expressing time.

CHAPTER 7

Structure Plans

As YET structure plans as operative expressions of planning policy exist in concept but not in reality.[1] Many structure plans are currently under preparation and that will continue after April 1974 when the responsibility for structure plans will pass to the new county authorities.[2] But no structure plan has yet been subjected to the principal test for a policy statement, which is the effectiveness with which it can bring policy to bear on executive decision making. Such decisions and actions are still being taken in relation to the current county and town maps and such other non-statutory plans and resolutions as exist to supplement them, though undoubtedly the ideas which underlie the structure plan as a policy statement have imbued the interpretation of these existing policy statements. Nevertheless, the main sources of guidance on the purposes, form and content of structure plans as policy statements remain for the present the Town and Country Planning Act 1971 itself and the closely related instructions and advice in the published Regulations,[3] Memorandum[4] and Manual,[5] together with such experience as has been gained in the preparation of structure plans to date[6] including the experience of the Greater London Development Plan, in some ways a forerunner of the structure plans.[7]

From these sources it is possible to determine the role which structure plans could potentially play in the overall environmental policy framework and the way in which the provisions regarding the form and content of structure plans affect that role, in particular, regarding the range of areas and topics, the emphasis on strategic policy, the associated choice of language and the expression of time.

FUNCTIONS OF STRUCTURE PLANS

The structure plan may be regarded as fulfilling five main functions as a policy statement:[8]

(i) *Interpreting national and regional policies*

Local authority policy making proceeds within a context set by central government through its management of the economy, including partial control over local authority capital and revenue expenditure, and its social and environmental policies;* more specific contexts to local authority policy may be set in regional development policies, including those made co-operatively between local and central government and given expression in an adopted regional strategy.[9] Both national and regional policies will be relatively generalised and their implications will need expressing in relation to local circumstances.

(ii) *Stating objectives and strategic policy*

The structure plan should contain a statement of the local authority's political objectives for the area and the strategic policies for environmental change which it is adopting in pursuit of these objectives.

(iii) *Stating policy norms for strategic promotional and regulatory decisions*

Some important executive decisions and actions will derive guidance direct from the structure plan where they are in response to strategic issues. The structure plan will need to contain some fairly direct expressions of desired relations for these limited issues to be secured by the local authority's promotional or regulatory powers.

(iv) *Providing a framework for detailed policy statements*

But the majority of executive decisions and actions will be guided by more detailed policy statements in local plans and programmes. The structure plan can indicate the kinds of topics or areas for which these detailed policies will be needed and the relationships between these and its strategic policies; in particular it must indicate action areas and broadly the kind of policy to be pursued in them.

(v) *Bringing major issues and policies before the public and the Secretary of State*

The opportunities for participation and objection provided with structure plans and the necessity of obtaining approval from the higher authority of the Secretary of State for the Environment create a means of bringing the

* See Chapter 2.

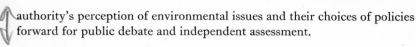authority's perception of environmental issues and their choices of policies forward for public debate and independent assessment.

PLAN AREAS

Structure plans should be prepared by local planning authorities for their administrative areas or, with the agreement of the Secretary of State, for parts of their area.[10] The Secretary of State has powers of direction on the timing of the submission of structure plans which could be used to secure contemporaneous submissions of neighbouring plans and further provisions have been made for the voluntary joint preparation and submission of structure plans by local planning authorities.[11] All these provisions recognise that administrative areas may not be the most appropriate areas for expressing planning policy, which may be better related to parts only of an administrative area or to the area of two or more planning authorities; to a lesser extent this is still likely to be the case with the new counties. In general terms the basic areal unit of the structure plan is likely to most usefully be the subregion as an area requiring closely related policies on functional and locational issues, including transport policy. Where such subregions cannot be readily defined or very easily or acceptably made the basic area for the structure plan, greater reliance must be placed on the regional context of the plan[12] or on the development of an agreed subregional framework by which commonly agreed policies for the subregion as a whole might be expressed in an individual authority's structure plan.[13]

But even though the structure plan relates primarily to a subregion it is still desirable to have regard to its component areas. The further development of policy, in more detailed local plans, will relate to subareas so that general consideration needs to be given in preparing a structure plan to the prospective pattern of local plans which will supplement it. This will need to be done in preparing the development plan scheme which will define the relative responsibilities of counties and districts for the preparation of local plans.[14] Beyond that, explicit consideration must be given to defining areas for which either Regulation 8 plans or action area plans are to be prepared. The provisions for Regulation 8 plans, presenting a supplementary policy statement in the form of a structure plan for part only of the area covered in broader terms by the main structure plan, are intended to relate to areas with major planning issues, likely to be true of urban areas of 50,000 population or more or smaller areas presenting particular classes of problem or opportunity.[15] The provisions for the identification of action areas in structure plans require a presentation of the location and extent of action areas in which proposals are to be commenced within 10 years of the submission of the structure plan to the Secretary of State, together with some broad indication of the kinds of policy to be expressed in detail in the subsequent action area plan.[16]

Apart from identifying these areas for which later, more detailed policy statements will supplement the structure plan, it may help the making and the expression of policy for the structure plan area as a whole to be divided into subareas.[17] Spelling out the implications of the broader, subregional policies for component areas, principally in verbal, descriptive terms, may be a useful device for presenting policies in terms which can be widely understood and which can inform public debate. The definition of areas for this purpose will relate to the kinds of issue with which the plan is chiefly concerned and the areas to which policy on these issues relate. They may therefore be large or small, defined in relation to very variable criteria. The amount of coverage they may need in the structure plan will likewise be variable.

THE RANGE OF POLICY

The structure plan is intended as a policy statement embracing the local planning authority's policy and general proposals in respect of the development and other use of land.[18] Development is defined to include, with certain exceptions, the carrying out of all building, engineering, mining or other operations on, over or under land, or the making of any material change in the use of any buildings or other land.[19] It embraces, therefore, all major changes in the use of the land resource and the constructional work associated with these changes. The one significant exception is changes in agricultural and forestry land use. In particular the development and other use of land should be construed as including measures for the improvement of the physical environment and the management of traffic, both of which are to be interpreted in the wide sense.[20] Under this broad umbrella the Regulations provide that policy in a structure plan should relate to such of the following as the local planning authority may think appropriate: population; employment; housing; industry and commerce; transportation; shopping; education; other social and community services; recreation and leisure; conservation, townscape and landscape; utility services; any other relevant matters.[21]

These requirements regarding the range of topics appropriate to structure plans can be interpreted narrowly or broadly. As a minimum a structure plan must concern itself with policy for controlling all those classes of change defined as development and therefore subject to planning control.[22] These include changes originating with the authority's own actions as a developer as well as changes initiated by other developers. This minimal extent of policy is essential if the development plan is to satisfy its function in guiding development control, for in exercising that control the local authority is enjoined to have regard to the provisions of the development plan so far as they are material to the application.[23] But potentially the structure plan can embrace a wider field of policy than the changes narrowly defined as development. It can serve as a statement of policy by which regulatory powers other than planning powers may be exercised in the control of environmental change: these include important powers to regulate traffic, housing accommodation and industrial processes to secure amenity, safety or public health. It can also serve as a basic statement of policy on the provision and management of those local authority services which make particular demands on land resources or which have strong influences on the development and use of land. Thus, for example, the structure plan should set out policies for the means of movement of people and goods by road, rail and other transport modes, whether under private or public operation and other provisions, in particular its land-use policies, should be related to these.[24] Likewise the plan may reflect the main lines of housing policy for the area, for the balance between conservation, improvement, redevelopment and new development and the timing of major housing changes under any of these heads will have important implications for the supply of building land and the pattern of transport movement.[25] On this wider interpretation the structure plan can become a comprehensive statement of objectives and environmental policy for an area. As such it would serve to guide executive decisions which the local authority makes under a variety of powers and procedures to control various kinds of environmental change.

This total field of environmental policy embraces all five policy fields of infrastructure, function, environmental quality, location and movement, and rate of change. Policy matters within these policy fields would be appropriate to the structure plan. Moreover, the relationship of this pattern

of policy fields to the elements in the activity and land resource systems and
to the kinds of issues with which planning has come to be concerned means
that this set of policy fields may provide a useful framework for the development and expression of structure plan policies.

STRATEGIC POLICY

Defining the range of concern of the structure plan in terms of areas or
topics is far simpler than defining the appropriate level of detail for the
expression of policies in structure plans. The structure plan is intended to set
out strategic issues and to express broad policies for dealing with them.[26]
It is a policy statement dealing only with matters affecting its area as a whole
or substantial parts of it.[27] The structure plan is clearly intended to be a
statement of strategic policy. It is concerned with policy for the minority of
the decisions which control a majority of the change in the activity systems
and their call on land resources. These are the decisions of which the
impacts are important marginal changes in the amounts or conditions of
activities, land uses, accommodations, movements, townscapes, landscapes
or other environmental attributes. The impact may be direct or it may be
indirect, consequential on chain reactions which cumulatively have major
impact. In either case the policy needed to guide decisions on changes of this
kind will be broader than could be given adequate expression in the more
tactical programmes or local plans, because they extend beyond the areal,
topical or time boundaries of such policy statements.[28] As statements of
strategic policy structure plans will be selective in their content and
generalised in their expression.

Even taking the broadest view of the range of policy appropriate to the
structure plan, that of environmental policy as a whole, not every decision
in this field is appropriate to the structure plan. For example, only those
decisions on the transport system which would significantly reorder travel
times and locational relationships, only those decisions on the townscape or
landscape which would significantly alter the character of large areas, only
those decisions on the housing stock which would significantly change its
profile will be the strategic elements. And in each case significance is to be
determined in terms of the scale of the change—in travel times, environmental character, housing availability—directly or indirectly brought about
by the decision. On this basis certain kinds of change will almost always raise

strategic issues, the choice of response will almost always need to be guided by strategic policy. So that the structure plan will normally need to contain policies regarding, for example, major marginal changes in basic employment, changes in the transport system, changes to the functions of town centres, changes in the provision of basic utility services, changes involving large land requirements, changes to the character of crests and ridges, changes including high or bulky buildings, changes in ambient air quality, and changes in the tenurial composition of the housing stock. These are all normally sensitive elements in the environment system as a whole. Other elements may be equally sensitive in local circumstances. Whatever the precise list of sensitive issues with potential strategic impact, these are the ones on which structure plan policy should be focused; other less strategic issues can be adequately handled in other policy statements.

In relation to such issues the structure plan will be concerned to define strategic policies which, like the chess strategy, will specify some broad policy relations between variables which still leave room for varied responses to individual issues as they arise. It must avoid too specific a definition of intent and its policies must therefore be fairly generalised in their expression. Its time span extends over a period of broadly 20 years ahead,[29] a period in which substantial aggregate changes will occur, but within this time span the plan is more likely to specify desirable quinquennial than annual rates of change. Likewise it will seek to relate policies for physical changes to approximate locations rather than specific sites—corridors rather than alignments for transport networks, zones rather than sites for land uses. And again the definition of policy variables by category will be generalised, relating, for example, to employment by blue collar: white collar, basic: non-basic kinds of distinction or possibly by industry groups but not referring to particular skills; similarly retail trade might be distinguished between convenience and durable goods, recreation between indoor and outdoor, group and individual, organised and casual activities; housing between single household and multi-household accommodation. It would be for tactical policy in local plans and programmes to make finer distinctions in all these cases—defining specific road alignments, site uses, shopping centre trade, recreation activities and housing provisions.

The relationships between variables to which structure plans give expression must also be generalised to a degree commensurate with the definition of the variables. Such relationships are more likely to be expressed in policy norms as relativities than as absolutes. The most absolute class of relationship, that of complements and incompatibilities, is likely to find only a limited application in the expression of strategic policy: for instance, when it seems desirable to put the force of the structure plan behind the preservation of a view, the mandatory provision of minor open spaces in residential developments or the replacement of housing accommodation upon redevelopment. But for the most part structure plan policy will seek to define the outer bounds of acceptable relations or acceptable exchange rates between what is desired. Thresholds and trade offs are therefore the most suitable classes of policy relation for the expression of structure plan policy, for they leave open to resolution in individual cases what the precise relationship between variables should be while expressing some limits of acceptability, adherence to which will secure policy objectives. The emphasis in the structure plan is therefore very strongly on the interrelationships between policies: interrelationships between topics—land use and transport, employment growth and housing availability, industrial change and air quality—and interrelationships between areas—residential and work areas, town centres and district centres, urban areas and recreation areas.[30] In its expression of these relationships, it is not the precise desirable relation which the structure plan expresses, but the broad order or nature of the relation.

This generality of expression influences too the language of structure plans. The plan is essentially a verbal statement of policy, supplemented by diagrams, tables, graphs and other illustrations. Its main illustration, the key diagram, shows the significant policies which have spatial expression. But it is not to be drawn on an Ordnance Survey base so that specific sites and locations are not identifiable on it, and it remains subordinate to the written statement of policy.[31] Two considerations lead to this emphasis on verbal statements of policy in the structure plan: the generality of structure plan policy which is more capable of expression through the richness of words than the precision of maps and formulas, and the function of the plan to set down issues for public debate which necessitates a form of expression which is widely comprehensible.

TIME IN STRUCTURE PLANS

The structure plan shares urban planning's concern with changes occurring over relatively long periods, a concern which is in part a reflection of some characteristics of the processes of change which planning seeks to control—the long lead times for development projects, the long life of urban infrastructure, the slow pace of much urban change and the particular nature of the land resource.* Thus the structure plan expresses policy for a period broadly of 20 years ahead, but without a fixed end date applicable to all its policies.[32] But the structure plan is concerned with changes likely to occur over the whole of this next 20 or so years, not just with the state of affairs likely to exist 20 years hence. That total period must therefore be broken down into short, medium and long term and separate regard paid to each; moreover, the relative emphasis on the subperiods will not need to be equal.

The structure plan can give expression to time basically in two ways, one in terms of the statistical basis of the plan, one in terms of the policy content of the plan.[33] Firstly, the basic forecasts can be related to the key census dates of 1971, 1981, 1991 for which the Registrar General's population projections will be available. Quinquennial projections are also likely to be needed, certainly in the short and medium term, and these must either be prepared locally or may be available from statements of regional policy, as in published regional strategies. The basic time frame for statistical purposes will then be something like 1971, 1976, 1981, 1986, 1991, 2001 with population, and possibly other variables, consistent with regional and national projections at 1971, 1981 and 1991 and possibly at 1976 and 1986 as well. Secondly, it will be desirable to identify approximately two kinds of key policy dates. There are those which mark the completion of a closely related sequence of changes, for example, the completion of development in an action area, the completion of the rundown of a particular source of employment, the achievement of a total coverage of smoke-control areas. There are also those which mark the initiation of a sequence of events likely to have many interactive consequences, some foreseen and allowed for in the structure plan, others which perhaps cannot be foreseen and must be the subject of contingency planning, for example, the insertion of a new link in a transport network such as a river crossing, the establishment of a major new source of employment, the removal of through traffic from a conservation area. In practice it may be hard to distinguish beginnings from endings in the continuous sequences of change in prospect, but it should be possible to identify approximately the key dates for structure plan policy at which

* See Chapter 5.

new strategic issues, currently latent, seem likely to arise. Some of these may have been brought together in the 10-year programme which may supplement the structure plan to make an assessment of progress in the 10 years following submission of the plan to the Secretary of State.[34] The key policy dates will not, except by coincidence, fit neatly with the statistical dates. But together they will provide the elements of a time frame for structure plan policy.

This time frame may be useful in developing either a static or a dynamic expression of structure plan policy. Both the key diagram and the 10-year programme can provide useful snapshots of where policy may have led by particular dates. Such snapshots are more generally comprehensible than statements of the policy relations by which the decisions which have produced that state of affairs have been guided. For the purpose of bringing issues and policies before the public the static expression of structure plan policy has its value. But it is essentially an expression of the likely outcomes of policy intended specifically for this one function. To serve the other functions of the structure plan a dynamic expression of policy, in terms of the relations between activities and between activities and resources which policy will seek to maintain over time or progressively change over time, is more suited to the strategic, comprehensive, long-term nature of structure plan policy. With the time span of structure plan policy such dynamic expressions of policy can only be more towards the Lewis and Clark variety,* in which the likely key policy dates and the policy relations which should guide executive decisions on a course between these dates are determined. The specificity with which it is possible to define the key dates, the courses between them and the relations needed to remain on course must diminish through the 20-year period as a simple consequence of increasing uncertainty about prevailing facts and values in the future.

But this increasing uncertainty does not matter so much. Although it is concerned to express policy for up to 20 years or more ahead, the structure plan must be more concerned with the 0–5-year shorter-term and 5–15-year medium-term periods than with the 15–25-year long-term period. This is not just because it is possible to build policies upon greater certainty in the shorter and medium term, but also because it is unnecessary for policies to be fixed in the longer term, since the executive decisions which present policies are to guide are all to be taken in the short–medium term. In

* See Chapter 5.

practice, major changes occurring within the short term, particularly developmental changes with their long lead times, are the outcome of the decisions taken in the recent past governed by policies prevailing then. Equally, the major executive decisions taken in the short term will generally produce outcomes in the medium term. It is therefore the medium-term period of 5–15 years from base year upon which the policies in the structure plan should be concentrated. In relation to the medium term, the short term and the long term have different significances. The changes already in train in the short term provide the base position on which new or revised policy can build, though it is not inconceivable that existing commitments to short-term change may appear so unsatisfactory in their consequences for the medium term that reconsideration is essential. But this will normally be an exception. The long term is significant for the opposite reason, that it provides a variety of long-term directions in which medium-term change might lead, none of which at the present can be regarded as finally preferable to the others though provisional orders of preference may be defined. Structure plan policies for the medium term are therefore needed to guide decisions on changes from the relatively known short-term position in directions that leave open for the present a choice of longer-term futures.

STRUCTURE PLANS AND CORPORATE PLANNING

Regarded as a plan prepared to give expression to medium term, strategic policy for subregions, the structure plan must be a significant policy statement when set in the context of the total policy needs of the local authority. In parallel with the changes which have been made in the development plan system to achieve the substitution of the structure and local plans for the 1962 Act development plan, there has been a movement towards improved policy making processes throughout all the policy fields of local authorities. To this end there is a growing movement to strengthen explicit policy making and explicit guidance of executive decisions by policy in fields where hitherto this has been implicit or weak. At the same time there is a striving towards better integration of policy right across the authority to improve urban policy as a whole, for social and economic as well as environmental affairs.

There is clearly in these circumstances the possibility of a conflict between the statutory development plan, particularly the strategic structure plan, and the corporate plan in whatever form it takes. It is clear that neither can the structure plan act as the corporate plan in any of its possible forms nor can the two kinds of statement stand independently of each other. The structure plan cannot give expression to all the local authority's policies because, even on the widest interpretation of its range extending quite beyond policy for changes regulated executively under the powers of the Town and Country Planning Acts to embrace environmental policy as a whole, it is still restricted statutorily to policies related to the development and other use of land and administratively to what the Secretary of State for the Environment has responsibility to approve. Many of the decisions and actions of a local authority, particularly in response to issues arising with social, life style changes and in the internal management of its financial and manpower resources, lie outside these limits. At the same time the structure plan cannot comfortably exist alongside a separate corporate plan: to be prepared independently would be wasteful of scarce manpower in the duplication of work and the end result would be confusing if not informed by common objectives and assumptions and comprising agreed and related policies. Economy in effort and avoidance of conflict would not be served this way.

Both these extreme and unattractive options are avoidable if attention is withdrawn from the concept of the corporate *plan*. In practice, the concept of the structure plan, its form and content, is more strongly defined by statute than the concept of its related plan or policy making process, apart from the procedural requirements governing consultation, including participation and rights of objection.* In contrast, with corporate planning the concept of the plan in terms of form and content is very weakly developed, a variety of concepts exist,† and the emphasis is strongly on the corporate nature of the plan or policy making process. A possible relationship between the structure plan and corporate planning is therefore to regard the statutory structure plan as one of the statements of policy derived from a corporate policy making and review process. There would then be, particularly for strategic policy, one central policy making process in a local authority and through this would be developed policy statements of various kinds, certainly the structure plan as a statement of strategic environmental policy, but also possibly social plans and economic plans, concerned respectively

* See Chapter 10.
† See Chapter 6.

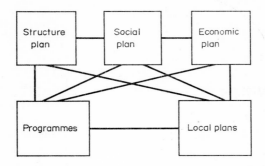

FIG. 7.1. Policy framework with additional strategic plans.

with guiding the authority's response to issues arising through changes in life style[35] and investments. The policy framework might then take the form illustrated in Fig. 7.1. This central policy making process would also provide a context for more detailed policy work, which in its turn would be given expression in more detailed policy statements including programmes and local plans. The corporate plan might then not exist, except as the sum of these separate policy statements, but the integration of the statements would have been secured by their derivation from a common process.

CHAPTER 8

Programmes

ONE of the main functions of the structure plan is to provide a framework for the further development of more detailed policy in other kinds of policy statements. Where the structure plan is regarded broadly rather than narrowly, as a statement of strategic environmental policy, and where it is prepared through a corporate policy making process in the local authority, then the further development of policy will find expression not simply in the local plans which are part of the 1971 Act development plan system but also in what might be termed programmes.

The distinction drawn between local plans and programmes in the environmental policy field are twofold. Firstly, while local plans relate essentially to a subarea, expressing policy on a range of topics as it relates to that area, programmes are concerned with one topic throughout the whole area of the local authority. The former has a predominantly areal basis, the latter a predominantly topical basis. This may not in some cases be a very fundamental distinction since the policy needs for a particular topic may have a restricted areal coverage: policy on mineral working would be an example of this. For topics of this kind the subject plan as a type of local plan exists and there will be occasions on which a choice between a subject plan and a programme statement of policy must be made.* The second distinction between local plans and programmes is more clear cut: local plans are statutory policy statements, their form, content and preparation subject to statutory provisions, whereas programmes are non-statutory. Nevertheless, programmes will relate closely to various formal, if non-statutory requirements, notably budgeting and investment programming. The basic distinctions are, however, between local plans as statutory, multi-topic policy statements for subareas and programmes as non-statutory, single-topic statements for whole areas: in more concrete terms, for example, between the town centre action area and the housing programme.

* See Chapter 9.

FUNCTIONS OF PROGRAMMES

Unlike structure and local plans there is no statutory source from which the functions of programmes can be derived. They can, however, be summarised as:

(i) *Applying the strategy of the structure plan*

The structure plan's comprehensive statement of objectives and of strategic environmental policy will have clear implications for particular programmes; these programmes will need to conform generally to strategic environmental policy. Some particular programmes may also in part be applying strategic social or economic policy.

(ii) *Stating detailed programme area policies*

In each programme a more detailed statement of policy will be developed for that particular topic, for both the authority's regulative and promotional decisions and actions.

(iii) *Detailing resource implications of programme area policy*

The framework of programme areas and the policy statements for them provide the link with resource management, both of medium term financial and manpower planning and of annual budgeting.

These functions will in turn have influence upon the pattern of programme areas, the level of detail in programmes and their treatment of time.

PROGRAMME AREAS

The necessity of finding some system of topics by which to systematise the entire field of environmental policy arises even more fundamentally with programmes than with structure plans. There the need was essentially to find a system which enhances understanding of issues and the presentation of policy; the emphasis was nevertheless on the comprehensive whole. With programmes some degree of separate execution of policy is an additional consideration so that it becomes necessary to temper functional with pragmatic considerations.

Functional considerations nevertheless provide a useful baseline in determining programme structures.[1] These functional considerations are an amalgam of two closely related matters: on the one hand, the elements and changing relationships among the activities and resources which the authority seeks to control, and, on the other hand, the objectives of the local authority and the kinds of issues which those objectives lead them to recognise. These are related through the mutual interactions of fact and value. These interactions underlie the complexity of developing an adequate functional programme structure. At all points difficult choices have to be made. When does pollution-control change from being public health oriented to being amenity oriented? Is highway building directed principally to improving environmental quality, minimising travel time or increasing economic growth? Do conservation policies help promote tourism? Such choices cannot be determined in principle but only in relation to actual cases. Nevertheless, within the environmental policy field it is likely that a programme structure related to local circumstances will have fairly identifiable within it the topics already defined:* the provision of adequate infrastructure of accommodation and utilities, the maintenance of environmental quality, the improvement of locational relationships through land use and transport changes, and the maintenance of the local economy.

Three other kinds of consideration may modify the functional programme structure: statutory powers and procedures, professional skills and traditions, and the allocation of local government functions. It can be argued that functional programme structures should not be distorted by these kinds of consideration. Certainly any departure from the pure approach weakens the use of the programme structure as an analytical device. But even for analysis, the constraints of available data and techniques on identifying expenditure and income, let alone social benefits, in relation to purely functional programme structures have to be faced. When the programme structure is also to serve as a framework for the executive promotion and regulation of change, then these other pragmatic considerations must be given added weight.

Powers and procedures for executive action in the environmental field have developed until recently within a traditional but implicit system of policy fields, related somewhat to what was the allocation of responsibility among both central and local government departments. Thus there have developed important separate codes of public health, town and country planning, transport and housing legislation, together with general local

* See Chapter 5.

government legislation and a variety of miscellaneous powers and procedures which lie outside these five fields.[2] In this way somewhat different powers have arisen for dealing with comparable problems, for example, industrial and vehicle noise;[3] and different procedures exist side by side, for example, for authorising site development and authorising highway development.[4] Equally important, differing patterns of relationship have developed between central departments and local authorities in the different fields. This applies particularly to the form taken by central government grants and loans and the form of central government authorisation of local authority capital investment, and also to requirements for central government approval of local authority policy statements in particular environmental policy fields. All of these add up to a complex pattern of powers and procedures in the environmental policy field. More recently some rationalisation has occurred in a number of directions. The departmental reorganisation which created the Department of the Environment put most parts of central government concerned with environmental policy under one Secretary of State.[5] The move toward simplified financial support systems for local authority functions, particularly in the replacement of specific by block grants and revenue by capital grants, has tended likewise to assist more aggregated views of policy.[6] And what were hitherto inconsistencies in either powers or procedures with regard to related or similar issues are being reduced by the progressive acceptance of environmental policy as a coherent field of administration, evident, for example, in the increasing association of policies on air pollution, water pollution and land dereliction, or at a more refined level in increasingly consistent policy on noise pollution from diverse sources.[7] In principle, environmental policy powers and procedures should be shaped to serve the programme structure rather than vice versa, but time lag in institutional adaptation is inescapable. So that some regard must be had to a largely historical pattern of powers and procedures in framing programme structures.

Some of these traditional fields of environmental policy have had long associations with particular professions with their ideologies and skills. This has been particularly true in local government where the professionalism of departments has been particularly strong, with conventionally, for example, separate engineers', architects', planners', medical officers', treasurers' and other departments. This close association of professionalism and policy field has frequently been a strength in the development of policy in the past;

those policy fields without a clearly related profession to support them have probably suffered in consequence. At the same time, too narrow a professionalism is also a source of weakness in identifying policy needs and devising effective, frequently cross-professional policies in response to these needs. So many of the issues with which environmental policies and programmes must be concerned do not lie neatly within the fields of concern of individual professions, nor are the responses to them ones to which the skills of single professions are exclusively relevant. Problems are rarely planning, architectural, engineering, medical or financial problems. More commonly they touch on all of these. A functional approach to programme structures is a recognition of this fact. Some local authorities have gone further to reorganise their departmental structures also in recognition of this fact. But professionalism remains a factor to consider in programme structures. The particular perceptions and skills which individuals involved in policy making bring to the task are conditioned to some degree by their professions. So that some kind of relationship between the pattern of professional skills and the pattern of programme areas is necessary.

Lastly the allocation of local government executive responsibilities between different classes of authority must be considered. The pattern of allocation will be altered substantially by the provisions of the Local Government Act 1972 which introduces county and district authorities throughout the country,[8] and by the parallel reorganisation of water authorities.[9] Some fields of policy which might on functional grounds be related to others within the overall environmental policy fields will fall outside the responsibility of particular local authorities, so that other means of associating policy than inclusion within the same programme area will have to be found. Within the overall field of environmental policy, responsibilities for executive action are to be either exclusively allocated to districts or counties, predominantly allocated to one or the other or allocated to both to be exercised concurrently in pursuit of agreed policy.[10] The basic pattern is shown in Table 8.1. These new allocations of executive responsibilities reflect a number of considerations including the size of area, the level of resources needed to exercise a function effectively, the efficient utilisation of specialised skills and a desire to place as many services as possible with the more local district authorities. Close links between executive functions may also have been a consideration but not necessarily a predominant one. As a consequence this particular allocation of responsibilities poses a further

TABLE 8.1. FUTURE ALLOCATION OF ENVIRONMENTAL
EXECUTIVE RESPONSIBILITIES

DISTRICTS	COUNTIES
Land use and development	Land use and development
	Highways
Public transport	*Public transport*
Parking	Parking
Building standards	
	Waste disposal
Air pollution	
Derelict land	Derelict land
Coast protection	
Building preservation	Building preservation
Tree preservation	Tree preservation
Housing	Housing
Land acquisition	Land acquisition
Parks and open space	Parks and open space
Advertisements	
	National parks
Country parks	Country parks
Town development	Town development
Footpaths	*Footpaths*

Note: Italics indicate exclusive or predominant powers, lower case indicates subsidiary or shared powers.

set of constraints on the formation of functional programme areas for the expression of policy.

Underlying the pragmatic constraints which these patterns of legal powers, professional skills and executive responsibilities impose on the adoption of a purely functional pattern of programme areas lies a fundamental point. It is that the considerations which determine a functional pattern of executive actions may not be the same as those which determine a functional pattern of policy fields or programme areas. In executive action the constraints of responsibilities, powers, skills and resources available to the authority are important and inescapable. They may be less so for policy making which is concerned in part with finding new ways of directing executive action, relating more closely actions which have hitherto been unrelated. At the same time policy must be expressed in terms which have meaning and relevance for executive decision making. This applies particularly to the range of policy in programmes focusing upon a particular topic.

For this reason the structure of programme areas must be a compromise, related on the one hand to the objectives of policy, on the other to the pattern of executive decisions.

TACTICAL POLICY

Programmes are statements of tactical policy to implement the strategy expressed in the structure plan. They take their context from the structure plan in two ways. Firstly, the structure plan provides a framework of basic objectives and strategic policies of a generalised and selective kind. The programme will develop these policies in more detail, as more precise proposals or standards or capital projects. But because of the selective nature of strategic policy in the structure plan it will need to supplement these statements with others which found no expression in the structure plan but which are necessary components of an overall programme area policy. Secondly, comprehensive policy in the structure plan should have expressed the main relations between the variables which are at the core of the different programme areas. Programme area policy can then be developed in the context of the structure plan in the confidence that its compatibility with policy development in other programme areas, at least in broad terms, is assured. In this way, for example, detailed transport policies can be developed within the context of a structure plan which has established satisfactory broad relationships between land use and transport; equally, detailed land assembly programmes can be developed on the basis of the structure plan which will have assured the broad freedom of those areas from air pollution and the availability of water and sewerage services. There will inevitably be more local interactions between programme area policies to be considered and local plans will have a useful role here in presenting the resolutions as subarea policies. But acceptance of the context of the structure plan should mean that satisfactory broad interactions have been determined.

Some programmes will also be implementing social and economic strategies as well as the environmental strategies of the structure plan. In those cases similar relationships between tactical programmes and social and economic policy statements analogous to the structure plan will exist. Some programmes will then sit astride the boundary between environmental and social affairs or between environmental and economic affairs. On the first of these boundaries housing will probably be the programme area which poses the most difficult problems, for housing is at once a major element in the environmental system and a major element in household budgets, life styles and social satisfactions. On the second of these boundaries any programme concerned with local economic growth concerning issues of job opportunity, population structure, personal incomes and the tax base of the authority may not entirely satisfactorily be regarded as a field of environmental policy alone. In these ways the programmes may relate to all kinds of strategic policy statement, not the structure plan alone.

The precise form of tactical policy statement for a programme area will depend greatly on whether it is a policy field in which the authority is to play a predominantly promotional or regulatory role, whether executive action is essentially at the initiative of the authority itself, mobilising its own finance and manpower resources to secure some change in the environment, or whether executive action is essentially responsive to change originating in the community which the authority can only seek to regulate. Clearly in the former case rather more certainty and commitment can be brought to policy making than in the latter. Most programme areas will combine elements of both kinds of executive action. In housing, for example, the local authority is both a promoter and a regulator of change: it builds itself, partly by redevelopment and partly by development, it grants permissions for private development, it may induce private development by land acquisition and disposal as well as by the provision of utilities to sites and by mortgage advances, it also induces the improvement of the existing housing stock through improvement grants. In transport the authority is in the promotional role as provider of highways and parking but a regulator also of private parking and frequently of public transport services, as also of the land use changes which generate traffic and travel demand. In environmental protection there is again a mixture of roles: the authority is directly responsible for waste disposal and derelict land reclamation but regulative of air and noise pollution. In consequence of this mixed character most programmes will contain, apart from a statement of objectives and policy norms, a clear indication of how their promotional and regulatory powers will be used to maintain those norms.

The policy norms themselves are more likely to be expressed as incompatibilities, complements and thresholds than as trade offs.* Programme area

* See Chapter 4.

policy will typically embrace statements of projects to be undertaken, standards to be enforced, expenditures to be committed, targets to be met, all relatively firm expressions of intent. The projects may be for land acquisition or development; the standards may be construction standards, land use standards, accommodation standards or emission standards; the expenditures might be on staff, equipment, materials or buildings; the targets might relate to air or water quality, traffic congestion or recreational facilities. All of these represent specific relations between policy variables expressing either points or ranges of acceptable values. They also illustrate the potential in tactical programme area policy for a wider use of mathematical expression of policy in technical standards, project designs and expenditure proposals.

Where programme area policies involve the commitment of the authority's own resources, the programmes will provide a link between environmental policy and forward resource planning for the authority as a whole. Many local authorities have established rolling capital investment programmes extending up to 5 years ahead in which they seek to specify the capital projects including land and property acquisition that they envisage in that period and their timing. These capital programmes serve various purposes. They provide a means of checking the overall feasibility of the level of capital investment and its consequent loan charges, which the authority envisages. They also provide a means of generating the information needed by central government in its approval of individual projects or programmes. These approval procedures increasingly either require the submission of a rolling programme of projects, as happens with transport investment, or can operate effectively to the advantage of authorities planning capital expenditure ahead in this way. In policy fields in which the authority's own capital projects are an important element of tactical policy there are these strong advantages in a firm development of programme policy statements.

Some policy fields in which the authority's own initiatives play a prominent role may not be characterised by important commitments of capital but by big changes in revenue, in particular manpower costs. Capital and revenue payments are both uses of financial resources. They may also sometimes represent alternative responses to an issue: for example, the solution to a particular localised pedestrian road accident problem may be either to install new capital plant in the form of lights and barriers or to employ additional police or wardens. Policy in most programme areas will involve a combination of both capital and revenue commitments and forward resource planning must take both into account. By building on the foundation of programmes, which are both related to policy objectives and inclusive of both promotional and regulatory actions by the authority, a surer system of resource planning may be established.

In the shorter term resource planning in local authorities is associated with the process of budgeting.[12] Annual budgets draw together for the authority as a whole all items of expenditure and income for the year: expenditure on running services they provide, on payments they make by way of grant or loan, and on loan charges on money borrowed for capital investment, and income including fees and charges they levy, grants they receive from central government and revenue from rates. In doing this budgets are at one and the same time a plan setting out proposed priorities between different policy fields for the coming year, a forecast of likely expenditures and incomes that those decisions will create, an authorisation of those expenditures, charges and taxes and a yardstick against which to measure the actual outturn of expenditure and income. Among these purposes a distinction can be drawn between those which relate to the authorisation and control of expenditure and those which relate to policy making. Annual revenue budgeting is a more effective instrument of the former than of the latter.[13] Its short time span, its high degree of precision, its emphasis on expenditure rather than achievement make it an imperfect tool of forward financial planning. Nevertheless it has its narrower role still and this is one which it can more effectively play where there is a coherent set of programme policy statements on which to build.

All these kinds of resource management—capital investment programmes, revenue planning, manpower planning, budgeting—represent approaches to the development of policies for the maintenance of the capabilities of finance, powers and manpower on which an authority's continued effective operation depends. They are policies focused on relations internal to the authority, in distinction to the policies expressed through structure plans, programmes or local plans which are focused on relations external to the authority. But both kinds of relation are important since the authority's continued effective operation as a controller of environmental change depends on the maintenance of its internal viability.* The essential point of contact between internal and external policies is the programme, for it is

* See Chapter 4.

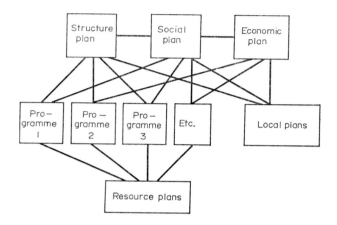

Fig. 8.1. Policy framework with programmes and resource plans.

there that the resource implications of external policy can be most extensively presented (see Fig. 8.1). Indeed, to detail these resource implications is one of the prime functions of programmes.

TIME IN PROGRAMMES

As the structure plan provides a context of objectives, policies and interactions in which detailed policy for particular programme areas can be developed, so it provides a temporal context. Whereas structure plans are concerned with the period extending up to 20 or more years ahead, programmes will rarely be concerned with developments beyond the short and medium term of the next 15 years. This follows from their greater detail and the corresponding increase in uncertainty which accompanies greater detail. But it is only possible to accept this shorter time span of concern in programmes because of the existence of the structure plan as a longer-term context. If short- or medium-term programme policy wishes to depart from the basic objectives or policies of the structure plan, then questions about the long-term acceptability of that new policy arise and must be considered in a review of the structure plan. Thus the structure plan does not take care of the long term in a way that makes any choice of medium-term policy tolerable; rather the absolution of programme policy from a longer term time perspective is only validated by its adherence to the basic framework of objectives and policies which the structure plan has set down.

While most are unlikely to be concerned with policy needs beyond 15 years ahead, different programme areas will differ in the period on which they need to focus: some will emphasise the short term more, some the medium term more. These differing degrees of emphasis will arise from the importance of the reasons for longer time perspectives in planning: where development projects are involved which have a long lead time, where land needs to be safeguarded for future uses, where the programme is creating infrastructure with an anticipated long life, or where benefits can only be expected in the longer term because of the slowness of the change which can be achieved—in all such circumstances there will be justification for programmes to extend their concern beyond the short to the medium term.

The key dates from the structure plan can provide the skeletal time frame for each programme. The statistical constraints applicable to the structure plan will apply equally and the key policy dates for major events in the structure plan are likely to be just as significant for the relevant programmes. But beyond that, linking the structure plan and the programme at the key dates will be an effective way of demonstrating that the programme relates to the structure plan as its context. But the programme will need to build more detailed timing on to this basic time frame. Whereas the structure plan was not expected in principle to be concerned with changes at less than quinquennial frequencies, the programmes are likely to need to work more towards an annual frequency of change. Where the focus is on the short term an annual coverage in the short term and a biennial, triennial or greater coverage in the later period might be appropriate. Where the focus is on the whole period of short and medium term a more even coverage would be appropriate.

But two additional considerations will influence this choice. Firstly, there will be the tactical equivalents of the structure plan's key policy dates, dates at which some significant sequence of changes originates or terminates. The greater specificity of programmes will mean that more key dates for policy can be set: for the completion of construction, for the eradication of some condition, for the achievement of some predetermined target. Targets of this kind will be an important expression of the objectives of tactical policy and they will need to be fixed fairly firmly in the temporal dimension. Secondly, in those policy fields in which local authority capital projects are an important element of policy and programme policy provides therefore an important input to financial planning, the necessity of building up capital investment programmes within the latter will add an extra requirement for time specification.

The programme as a policy statement will therefore be essentially expressing a dynamic approach to time, rather than a static one, focusing particularly on the sequence of changes which policy is seeking to secure within that programme area. Whether that sequence is expressed more in the Cook's Tour mould or more in the Lewis and Clark mould* will depend on the time period with which the programme is concerned—the Cook's Tour mould will be more appropriate where the focus is firmly on the short term —and on the extent to which the authority is the promoter or the regulator of change in a particular programme area—the Cook's Tour mould will be more appropriate to programmes of the former kind.

SOME POSSIBLE PROGRAMME AREAS

These characteristics of programme policy statements will be expressed in different degrees in different programme areas. The precise pattern of those programme areas cannot be specified in universal terms but must be developed to serve specific policy needs. The form and content of some possible programmes can, however, be briefly outlined to illustrate characteristics of programme areas in general. These illustrative programmes are for housing, environmental protection and transport.

A *housing programme* would take as its context not just the strategic environmental policies of the structure plan, but also to some degree strategic social policies of the authority. This is inevitable since housing is at one and the same time the chief physical component of the environment, the main class of accommodation for human activity, a major claim on household income and a key element in household satisfaction and stability. Whether housing programmes develop principally from environmental or social considerations or equally from both will depend very much on the kind of issues with which local housing policy needs to concern itself. These will clearly be different in a dense, long-developed area with a heterogeneous, relatively deprived population than in a new and rapidly developing subur-

* See Chapter 5.

ban area with a newly immigrant, relatively prosperous, young population. Both will have their problems but they will differ and the objectives of policy will likewise differ.

The issues with which the housing programme is concerned will relate to the whole housing market: the housing needs of all income groups and household types, the housing provision of private developers and housing corporations as well as the authority itself, the amount and quality of the housing and also its tenure, rent and price, the kind of housing units as well as their location. It must be a comprehensive housing policy informed by some overall understanding of how these elements interact.[12] It will be a means of marshalling a variety of resources, powers and skills within the local authority: resources of land and capital available to the local authority, with or without financial support from central government; powers to regulate development, to acquire land and property, to improve existing property or to build new housing;[13] skills of the architects, housing managers, lawyers, medical officers, planners, engineers and surveyors on the staff of the authority. Such a housing programme might have two subprogrammes concerned respectively with matching households with housing available and with changing the housing stock.

The first subprogramme would essentially be providing services to households. It would be advisory and allocative. The development and encouragement of housing advice centres would be an important basic organisational element of policy here. Such centres are intended to disseminate information on housing opportunities for all kinds of tenure within the area of the authority and outside, as well as on the various kinds of assistance available to households in the form of rent rebates and local authority mortgages. More specifically this subprogramme would be specifying the policies determining the availability, to both new households and households displaced by redevelopment, of local authority tenancies, local authority mortgages, houses for purchase from the local authority, temporary housing accommodation and, where appropriate, eligibility for overspill housing schemes. It might also be concerned with policies for the regulation of multi-occupied dwellings and the general maintenance of fitness in the housing stock.

The second subprogramme would essentially be concerned with mobilising resources needed to alter the size and content of the housing stock where the policies for matching households to housing available were inhibited by shortfalls of adequate housing. The inadequacies in the housing stock might be in terms of location, dwelling type, tenure type, rent or price level. The resources available to the authority are essentially those of land and capital. Increases in land availability depend in the first instance on planning powers for allocating land for housing development, ensuring that it can be serviced, particularly by highways and sewers, and then granting planning permission for residential use. Policies for the progressive release of land for housing will be an important component of the housing programme. It will be necessary to couple this with policies for the acquisition of land, certainly for the authority's own development, but in circumstances also for disposal to private developers or housing corporations. This might be done by the authority itself or in partnership with landowners or developers.[14] Where development or redevelopment is to be undertaken by the authority itself, additional capital resources must be mobilised for that development. Such redevelopment policies must be related to policies for house improvement, both by the authority itself and by owners with the assistance of grants and loans from the authority.

These programmes will stand in their own right as policy statements for the regulation of executive decisions, but they will also provide input for other kinds of statement. Housing is an important local authority service and a major claim on its financial resources. The housing programme will therefore feed into financial planning and budgeting. It will also incidentally provide a means of satisfying *ad hoc* requests for reports on progress from central government and the need to submit particular projects to central government for grant approval, although there is currently no requirement for the submission of capital housing programmes for approval. Furthermore, housing as an important element of the environment and user of land means that the housing programme, while reflecting the strategic environmental policies of the structure plan, must itself be reflected in local plans.

An *environmental protection programme* would give expression to policies for safeguarding air, water and land against degradation by the wastes which activities create. It would be concerned with policies for either controlling the sources of pollution or for mitigating its effects. It would take its context principally from the structure plan, but would also need to have regard to strategic policies for the economic development of an area for it would inevitably have impacts on the operation and competitive position of economic activities in an area and on the locational choices of immigrant enterprises and residents. It would also be characterised as a programme area by the involvement of a diversity of authorities—both counties and districts will have responsibilities in this field, as well as the proposed water authorities—and its reliance on a diversity of powers.[15] An environmental protection programme might have three subprogrammes dealing with air, water and land.

The air subprogramme would deal with air pollution and noise. It would set air quality and noise standards for the area and define policies for attaining them, where present conditions fall short of them, and maintaining them thereafter. The standards would be concerned principally with industrial, domestic and traffic sources of air pollution and industrial, traffic and aircraft sources of noise. The policies would be either of a zoning nature, defining areas in which either pollution generators, particularly industrial plants and highways, should and should not be located or relocated and areas in which pollution-sensitive activities, particularly residential areas, should and should not be located. Such zoning would be put into effect through the regulation of proposed new development and redevelopment, some of which, notably in the housing and highway fields, the authority itself would be undertaking. Policies for more direct action to require abatement of both noise and air pollution sources might be coupled with this to achieve some more immediate amelioration of existing conditions; such policies would define the circumstances in which restriction of existing activities to this end might be sought. This would include the definition of smoke-control areas in which, with financial assistance towards adaptation of existing appliances, restrictions on smoke emission would be applied.

The water subprogramme would deal with the safeguarding of water quality and supply through the control of abstraction from both surface and underground sources and the discharge of waste water and sewage. Its concern would be with the entire water cycle and such a subprogramme would primarily be the responsibility of the proposed regional water authorities. It would need to set standards of water supply and standards of water quality for all stages of the water cycle and to determine policies for abstraction and discharge appropriate to attaining and maintaining these standards. Such policies would need to embrace both direct control over the supply of water and discharge of waste water from activities as well as the regulation of the location and growth of development as it affects, for example, water-gathering grounds or already overloaded watercourses.

The land subprogramme would deal with the disposal on land of domestic and industrial solid waste or refuse, the regulation of mineral working and the restoration of derelict land: it is concerned then with all those processes which uncontrolled would leave land degraded without beneficial use. Policies in this area are concerned not with restrictions on the generation of pollutants but rather with the regulation of their disposal to minimise permanent degradation of land and to prevent damage to water supplies. They include the location and management of tipping grounds operated by the authority and by industry and waste disposal contractors and, where possible, policies to employ solid wastes for the reclamation of derelict lands and exhausted mineral workings. It might include the making of payments to assist the reclamation of derelict lands by these and other means. It would also embrace the regulation of the location and operation of mineral working both to minimise nuisance and to ensure where possible future beneficial uses for the land once mineral working ceases.

Of the policies coming within an environmental protection programme only those for water supply and sewerage and for derelict land reclamation require major commitments of capital. The others are of a more regulatory nature, supplemented in cases by minor capital investments or revenue payments. In water and sewerage and in reclamation this programme will provide significant inputs to forward resource planning in the authority and will provide a basis for the submission of capital programmes and projects for central government approval. Much of this programme is dependent on control over the location and form of development and these policies will find further expression in local plans.

A *transport programme* would probably take as its context from the structure plan an overall balance between modes by journey purpose, the policies need to maintain that and policies for the future developments of the transport system—roads, public transport and parking—related to the pattern of land use to which the structure plan committed the authority. Within that context the transport programme might define the desired performance levels more precisely and determine the management policies and the programme of development in terms of both manpower and capital. The transport programme would principally be the concern of a county authority, acting in concert with district councils and public transport operators, and built mostly on powers to provide facilities or services or to make payments to others to do so rather than on regulatory powers.[16] Such a transport programme might have two elements: an operations subprogramme and a system development subprogramme.

The first subprogramme would be concerned with the management of existing transport facilities. The core policies would be those for road-traffic management to obtain the most effective use of the road system by both private and public transport consonant with the environmental objectives expressed in the structure plan. This would be supplemented by parking-control policies for regulating private transport and by management policies on levels of service, coordination of services and fares for sustaining bus services, supported where necessary by payments towards operators' costs; where rail public transport is an element then similar policies would apply.

The second subprogramme would be concerned with proposals for the future development of transport systems within the area. Where tracked public transport was an element in the system then proposals for its extension or improvement would be part of this subprogramme. Otherwise it would be focused on the improvement of the road system, within the context of the pattern of the primary road system to which the structure plan gives expression, for which a phased sequence of changes down to and including local distributors might be included. This would be supplemented by proposals for new or improved terminals and vehicles for bus public transport and proposals for parking provision for private vehicles, including the policies needed to regulate provision of private parking space provided with new developments.

The transport programme in the future could be the Transport Policies and Programmes proposed as a basis for the payment of a transport block grant to county authorities by central government in substitution for the variety of specific capital grants currently paid.[17] Each Transport Policies and Programmes would consist of policies and proposals, including both capital and operating expenditure, over a period of up to 15 years covering the whole transport field of roads, public transport, parking, traffic management and the movement of goods. As well as this, transport programmes will have important consequences for local plans, particularly as it will be through their inclusion in local plans that proposals for the development of the highway network will be given detailed expression as a basis for the granting of planning permission.

The form and content of such housing, environmental protection and transport programmes are illustrative only. In some circumstances these topics might not come to be considered as programmes in this way. Nor are these the only programmes which would take their context principally from the structure plan: others might be a conservation programme covering both landscape and townscape and including policies on the definition of conservation areas, the uses of historic buildings, and on the conservation of landscape and public access to it; there might also be a recreation and leisure programme including policies for both indoor and outdoor recreational activities, also programmes for the economic development of the area or for tourism development. And in addition to these there would of course be programmes outside the environmental policy field, in education, welfare, public health and protection.

CHAPTER 9

Local Plans

As POLICY statements, statutory local plans like structure plans exist in concept but not in reality, for their formal adoption by a local planning authority is contingent on the prior approval of a structure plan and as yet no approved structure plans exist. In practice a lot of experience in both the preparation and operation of the local plan type of policy statement in planning has been gained through the widespread use of town centre maps, village plans and similar variants of informal plans. The statutory local plan is in many ways a formalisation of this practice. Apart from that experience, which has hardly been documented, the main sources of guidance on the form and content of local plans are, as with structure plans, the Town and Country Planning Act 1971,[1] the Regulations,[2] the Memorandum[3] and the Manual.[4]

Their statutory basis is one of the features which distinguishes local plans from programmes as tactical expressions of environmental policy. The other distinguishing feature is the areal basis for policy in the local plan compared with the topical basis of the programme. The local plan is, with the exception of the subject plan,* a comprehensive statement of policy for a restricted area. Both of these characteristics are of significance for the functions of the local plans in the overall system of policy statements.

Whereas the structure plan will be the responsibility of the post-1974 county authorities, and programmes may be either county or district responsibilities dependent on programme areas, the local plans are predominantly the concern of the districts. Authority to prepare local plans will rest with both counties and districts and an agreement known as a development plan scheme must be reached between them over their respective responsibilities for the preparation of local plans.[5] In practice county authority

* See below.

125

initiative may well be limited to two classes of local plan: those of particular significance for strategic structure plan policy and those which relate closely to the county's exclusive or predominant responsibilities for highways, public transport, solid waste disposal and national parks. The majority of local plans are likely to be prepared by the district authorities which will have the leading role in the executive control of environmental change.

FUNCTIONS OF LOCAL PLANS

The functions of local plans will be comparable to those of programmes in their relation to the structure plan but will differ in consequence of their areal basis and statutory nature. These functions can be summarised as[6]

(i) *Applying the strategy of the structure plan*

Local plans will develop the implications of structure plan objectives and policies for the particular areas for which they are prepared. They will need to conform generally to the strategic environmental policy of the structure plan and in the case of local plans prepared by districts certification of conformity by the county will be necessary.[7]

(ii) *Stating detailed local environment policies*

For any area in which significant changes are expected a more detailed policy statement will be useful, extending beyond the local implications of strategic policy to embrace the local expression of programme policies as well. The local plan then becomes a synthesis of policies for change within that area and thereby a basis for the regulation of development under development control or other regulatory powers and for the promotion and coordination of change, particularly developmental changes.

(iii) *Bringing local issues and policies before the public*

Just as the topical nature of programme area policy illuminates the resource implications of environmental policy, so the areal nature of local plans illuminates the consequences of policy for consumers, operators and developers by giving it a more concrete expression, related to specific locations and sites, thereby providing a firmer basis for participation and objection.

PLAN AREAS

Local plans are for areas smaller than those covered by structure plans. The structure plan may well identify some subareas to assist either the preparation or the presentation of its policies. Some broad pattern of local plan areas will have been derived from these considerations and, in particular, the location if not the precise boundaries of action areas will have been defined in the structure plan. These will provide a starting point for the definition of local plan areas.

There is no statutory obligation or practical necessity for a complete coverage of the structure plan area by subsequent local plans. There will in most circumstances be parts of that area in which the general policies of the structure plan, possibly supplemented by programme policies, provide sufficient statements of policy to guide executive decisions on the changes occurring in those areas, which might be either very restricted in number or very insignificant in their impacts. This is likely to be true of large areas of the countryside and of parts of urban areas in which stable patterns of activity predominate. But in other parts of the structure plan area in which change is more rapid or more fundamental in nature, local plans to supplement the structure plan and the programmes will be needed for those particular functions which local plans fulfil, especially the local synthesis of diverse policies and their exposure to the public for participation and objection. While some areas will have no local plans, others may have more than one. It is possible for different types of local plan to be prepared for different purposes for the same area: principally this means that some action areas will be further refinements of district plans while others will rest directly within the context of the structure plan.

This is possible simply because of the different intentions behind the district, the action area and the subject plans.[8] While the district plan is intended as a statement of comprehensive policy for relatively large areas, usually where change will take place in a piecemeal fashion over a long period of time, the action area plan is intended as a statement of comprehensive policy for intensive change over a short period of time which will in normal circumstances be in a more restricted area; and the subject plan is concerned with a particular class of change and extends spatially as far as that class does. Typically, therefore, a district plan might be applied to a town centre, possibly in this case with further detailed action area plans for

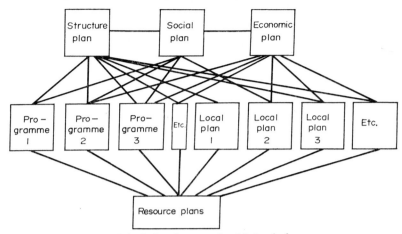

Fig. 9.1. Policy framework with local plans.

parts of it, an inner housing area undergoing renewal, a country town, a coastal or rural area of recreational and landscape value. An action area plan might be applied to a new highway with associated development, a country park, the expansion of an existing shopping centre. A subject plan might be applied to a land-reclamation project, the landscaping of a motorway corridor, the regulation of an area of mineral working.*

Plan areas for all three kinds of local plan can be defined in relation to the nature of the change with which the policies they express are concerned. For the subject plan the area should be that in which a particular class of change occurs. For district and action area plans it is the rate rather than the class of change which provides the criterion for delimiting the plan area: areas in which the issues arise from relatively rapid change, whether in the building stock, the activities it accommodates or the environment it creates, merit policy statements in the form of action area plans; areas in which the issues relate to less rapid change in one or more of these elements merit policy statements in the form of district plans. In most circumstances rapid rates of change are likely to be very localised given the incremental and marginal way in which environmental changes occur. Action area plans will therefore commonly relate to relatively small areas and the intensity of

* A variety of local plans will then stand alongside the variety of programmes in the overall policy framework (see Fig. 9.1).

PART THREE .

The Making of Policy

objectives. Any environmental change which maintains those norms is in accord with policy. Wide-ranging consideration of alternatives, forecasting of outcomes or complex comparisons of actions are not generally necessary in executive decision making to make it both rational and purposive, because it can relate its choice of action directly to policy.

The rationality and purposiveness of decision making in its entirety therefore rests on the process by which policy norms are determined, the process of policy making and review. In some policy making the require-ments of rationality and purposiveness may be relatively easily satisfied. For example, where policy relates to one element in a system, such as the location of a highway route or choosing between a slower or a faster rate of housing redevelopment in an area, the objectives may be known, the alter-natives easily defined and their outcomes forecast, and their comparison may lead to the clear preeminence of one, so that an unequivocal choice can be made. But for many planning policies the problem will be more difficult.[3] Each of the five requirements may cause difficulties. The objectives of policy may not be firmly fixed at the start: on the one hand, it may not be possible to determine those discriminatory objectives which are to be sought without some knowledge of the likely outcomes of alternatives which may attain them, and on the other hand, few mandatory objectives or constraints are absolute, most can be overcome at some kind of cost, the precise amount of which can rarely be known very exactly in advance. Moreover, there are boundary problems with alternatives in deciding how to handle alternatives lying outside the policy field under consideration or belonging properly to other kinds of policy statement or relating to the executive power of agencies not necessarily committed to a local authority's policy. There are problems of technique in predicting the likely outcomes of alternative policies and finding appropriate measures relative to objectives to use in the evaluation. Evaluation almost always involves to some degree the comparison of unlike measures since a common metric for all likely outcomes continues to elude decision making. And underlying all these problems there is the difficult relationship between technics and politics—of feeding technical work into political decision making and of infusing political values into technical work.

These difficulties indicate that the rational and purposive policy making model is both a simplification and an ideal.[4] But it is an ideal which must be pursued, principally because public authorities are accountable for their decisions to a wider interest than themselves. They are accountable to

the community, both to the community at large, through requirements for participation and rights of objection and ultimately through the electoral system, and to the many groups in the community—developers, operators and consumers—on whose acquiescence and actions the success of policy largely rests. For this reason 1971 Act development plans must contain a reasoned justification of their policies in relation to the social, economic and physical objectives of the community.[5] Purposiveness and rationality will be readily achieved in some fields of policy more than in others and in some kinds of policy statement more than in others. The paradigm of decision making must be developed differently in different circumstances. Strategic policy, with its lesser detail and greater uncertainties, will merit a different approach from tactical policy; short-term policy may be more realistically constrained than long-term policy; land use and transport policy with its fairly well-established theoretical base in location theory and a substantial body of technique must be tackled slightly differently from conservation policy where this base is almost completely lacking. Nevertheless common elements to the policy making or review process appropriate to all kinds of environmental policy do exist.

The three basic elements are the tasks of analysis, evaluation and consultation, each of which is always present to some degree in policy making in planning. They represent three strands from which a policy making process must be woven. By analysis is meant the task of understanding the working of the activity systems and their interaction with resources with which planning is concerned. But analysis alone is insufficient for policy making because planning policies are more than factual propositions about the nature of the environment. They certainly include or imply descriptions of a future state of the environment, but they possess in addition a normative quality by stating a preference for one state over another. So that evaluation is also necessary to bring this normative quality to policy making. By the task of evaluation is meant the determination of the appropriate ends and means of public action to control change in the environment subsystem. By the task of consultation is meant the process of seeking an agreement on those means and ends with those interests whose acquiescence to them is needed. Governments exist to serve the public interest and they also dispose of coercive powers not available to private agencies. For these reasons public policy making is commonly bound by rules or conventions of publication, consultation, objection and appeal which have no parallel outside.[6]

the context is much more restricting. At the same time, within a given context, the objectives defined for policy should be sufficiently broad that no major alternative at that level of policy is excluded and yet sufficiently detailed that the outcomes of alternatives can be related to them by fairly precise measures.

The definition of objectives is essentially a process of reviewing objectives which underlie current operational policies, and which are either explicit in current policy or implicit in past executive decisions. Dissatisfaction with present policy is the common starting point for policy review. The failure of present policy will become apparent in failing responses to issues, more particularly in failures to solve problems or failures to exploit opportunities. Such failures will arise from the inadequate knowledge or inappropriate values on which policy is based. Where the latter is the case, dissatisfaction may extend from the policies to the objectives which they serve, and review of objectives then becomes as important as the review of policies. The sources of revised objectives for policy lie in those same five fields—through changes in statutory obligations, central government influence, community pressure, professional or political ideologies—which determine the authority's willingness to recognise an issue for executive response*—

(i) the statutory obligations of the authority to respond to certain classes of situation which hitherto lay outside their competence: these should be set out quite clearly in the statutes, regulations and circulars of central government;

(ii) the context of national and regional policies; these may be expressed somewhat explicitly in published documents, for example, in regional planning strategies or public expenditure forecasts, but just as frequently will only be implicit in executive decisions which have been taken and therefore require interpretation and elucidation;

(iii) the values held by the community, to be ascertained through consultation procedures, participation exercises or attitude or behavioural surveys;

(iv) professional ideologies, largely the unique contribution of the professional staff itself;

(v) political ideologies, which will achieve some ultimate expression in

* See Chapter 3.

the final political choice between means and ends, but which it might be possible to establish in principle at an earlier stage.

From such sources a coherent set of objectives can be established for use in the matrix.

For a given set of objectives alternatives represent a lower level expression of means to achieve them. The definition of means must therefore follow on from that of ends. It must also be undertaken with regard to those ends which are constraints, that is objectives of which the attainment is mandatory as a condition of the feasibility of the alternatives. The objectives to be attained and the constraints to be satisfied therefore provide boundaries for what can be termed the policy space which is the field in which all the possibilities for policies lie. The task of defining alternative means is a search inside this space.[10]

Again the view of policy making as essentially policy review provides a starting point in current policies. Current policies, unless totally unrelated to the newly defined objectives and constraints, represent one of the alternatives for consideration for two reasons. Firstly, because there should be a predisposition towards continuity in public policy, in recognition of the disbenefits flowing from a change in policy, especially the write-off of various kinds of commitments, which must be offset by the benefits from the new policy to make change worth while. Secondly, consideration of the present and likely future outcomes of existing policy provides useful indications of the directions in which new policies can be sought. But beyond this starting point, the devising of further policy alternatives is essentially an innovative task.

Two elements seem essential to policy innovation. The first is a disaggregation of the policy space to explore in more detail the potentialities of its component parts.[11] This is essentially part of the analytical strand of work Such disaggregation can be undertaken from various perspectives: for example, from a capital resource perspective in an analysis of the allocation of resources under present policies, the proportion of future resources committed to maintaining present commitments and the size of the residue left between this sum and the overall capital resource constraint applicable;[12] from a locational perspective by techniques such as sieve maps threshold analysis and potential surface analysis which seek to define areas for development of varying degrees of potential;[13] or from a social perspec tive by social area analysis which seeks to identify the characteristics of different subgroups within the community and the policies which would be needed to ameliorate or sustain them.[14] The second element is the skill of creativity—the ability to envisage in the mind what has not yet been experienced in reality.[15] In particular this occurs through the rearrangement in imagination of the disaggregated items which have been identified, so as to see them in a changed relationship and another context.[16] To some such process of disaggregation and reaggregation, policy innovations as diverse as pedestrianised streets, staggered working hours, countryside access agreements or out of town shopping centres have come into existence.

Predicting the outcome of alternatives relative to objectives rests on an understanding of the processes of change in the environment system sufficient to enable predictions of some reliability to be made. This is again one of the tasks of analysis. From such predictions performance measures must be drawn for insertion in the cells of the matrix. A basic distinction can be made between measures of cost, expressing the capital resources consumed, and measures of benefit or disbenefit, expressing the positive or negative utility thereby derived. Ideally all measures should be quantified and in commensurable form: monetary measures, though the hardest to devise, provide the readiest means of satisfying these requirements, but other scores or rank orders based on subjective preferences might be used. The measures of cost and benefit need associating under each alternative with particular objectives, and additionally account needs to be taken of the incidence of outcomes over time, distinguishing shorter- from longer-term costs and benefits and valuing them differently according to some time preference.[17]

Like the related analytical problem of prediction, the problem of defining suitable measures for use in evaluation is very severe, though differing in severity for different kinds and levels of policy. Spurious measures will be more misleading than simple verbal statements but, while avoiding the spurious and employing some imagination in the use of proxies, much can be achieved in defining appropriate performance measures for particular objectives within the limitations of what predictions can be made.[18] Nevertheless, the final matrix will inevitably be mixed in its content as Fig. 10.2 illustrates. That this is so is an inescapable consequence of changes in the needs of policy making in planning, for as rapidly as techniques for adequate prediction and commensurable measurement are developed the objectives to which policy is directed become widened and new outcomes,

	A		B		C		D		E		
	Costs	Benefits	Costs	Benefits	Costs	Benefits	Costs	Benefits	Costs	Benefits	
1	£	£	£	£	£	£	£	£	£	£	Monetary measures
2	2		1		3		5		4		Rank scores
3	£ good		£ poor		£ bad		£ good		£ v good		Verbal
4	85		70		48		87		91		Physical measure
5	£ 20		£ 21		£ 18		£ 28		£ 19		Mixed

FIG. 10.2. Matrix with mixed measures.

hard to predict and measure, become a desired component of the matrix.[19] The mixed matrix problem is therefore always likely to exist in planning policy evaluations.

Completion of the matrix with objectives, alternatives and measures of predicted outcomes provides a basis for various ways of manipulating it to provide interpretations of the outcomes and thereby insights into the characteristics and performance of the alternatives and the objectives. Some of these manipulations are desirable to overcome the problems of mixed matrices, in particular to achieve greater degrees of commensurability, others are necessary to yield conclusions on the overall performance of alternatives from different viewpoints. The particular manipulations to be undertaken must depend on those aspects of the alternatives considered most important in the choice between them. The emphasis will vary with the type of policy statement under preparation or review: in this respect structure plan evaluation must differ from local plan evaluation, district plan evaluation from action area evaluation, programme evaluation between different programme areas. But there are only four basic aspects from which the alternatives can be considered: effectiveness, resource utilisation, distributional effects and response to uncertainty,[20] each deriving from some characteristic of policy, of the nature of the environment system or of the institutions of government.

Effectiveness concerns the degree of achievement of objectives, either solely on the basis of benefits or disbenefits or considering the related commitment of resources as well. In this latter case it becomes cost-effectiveness. Greater effectiveness is one of the main rationales for the existence of policy.* But considerations of effectiveness are likely to be more important in the more normative kinds of policy making, particularly for strategic policy with its less constrained context. Even a mixed matrix can be used to compare the effectiveness of alternatives objective by objective by reading across the rows to compare the alternative combination of costs and benefits relative to one objective or reading down the columns to inspect the association of costs and benefits relative to different objectives in each alternative. In this way possible ways of improving the effectiveness of alternatives through modification of them or of objectives may be indicated. Beyond this the mixed matrix may be reduced to commensurable form to enable summation into measures of overall effectiveness through ranking, normalising or weighting the elements of the matrix: ranking means substituting rank orders of preference for the disparate measures of outcome; normalising means instead substituting scores on a scale; weighting means attaching weights to the objectives and the outcome measures to indicate the relative worth of their attainment. While such techniques provide a basis for aggregation, at the same time they introduce assumptions which restrict the interpretation of the results.[21]

Resource utilisation concerns the claim on capital resources and the returns on resources which alternatives present. Any local authority must be mindful of the effect of its external policies, particularly through commitments of capital and changes in its tax base, on those internal relations which maintain its financial viability.† Where policy review is undertaken subject to capital resource constraints, either overall or sectoral, the necessity is to sum the cost columns and compare them with the constraints which have been defined. Where the kind of policy under review necessitates considerations additional to the call on capital, such as considerations of financial feasibility, then the likely revenues each alternative might yield as benefits, for example, in rates, rents or other payments, can be considered as financial returns to set against capital and recurrent costs. Some policies, particularly those involving detailed capital investment projects, may merit concern with the

* See Chapter 3.
† See Chapter 2.

social return on capital, achieved by expressing all relevant benefits in monetary terms and aggregating both costs and benefits to a summary measure of rate of return, benefit–cost ratio or net present value.[22]

Distributional effects concerns the incidence of costs and benefits within the community, determining who pays and who benefits from the different policy alternatives. This aspect is important because of the basic concern with equity in a democratic political system.* Where these considerations are particularly important, which is likely to be for short–medium term policies on which public interest particularly focuses, the basic matrix must be developed into a series of submatrices for affected subgroups of developers, operators or consumers, including central and local government as they act in these capacities. The submatrices can show the pattern of cost and benefits as they fall upon these groups and can be compared one with another and with the mean distribution.

Response to uncertainty concerns the degree to which alternatives are either resistant to unforeseen change, have qualities of robustness, or are capable of adaptation to such change, or have qualities of flexibility.† Uncertainty is always a consideration in decision making, but is particularly significant for planning in view of the partial control over environmental change which the authority can exercise and the relatively long term time span of planning policy. These considerations will matter more where the policy under review is longer term, since uncertainty increases into the future, or closely related to highly uncertain variables, for example, national economic trends, over which the local authority has little or no control. The definitions of objectives will have rested upon assumptions about the continued validity of values, the definition of alternatives and the prediction of their outcomes will have rested upon assumptions about the future likelihood of certain facts or events. Those sets of assumptions will almost certainly to some degree be wrong. The matrix can be manipulated to consider the consequences of variations in these assumptions through sensitivity analysis, by varying the assumptions underlying the alternatives and their outcomes to provide alternative columns of consequent costs and benefits, or by varying the assumptions about the weighting of objectives to provide alternative rows of consequent costs and benefits. From this it becomes possible to identify sensitive cells of the matrix indicating alterna-

* See Chapter 3.
† See Chapter 5.

tives or objectives in which uncertainty is a significant factor and for which a high degree of flexibility or robustness is desirable.

Such manipulations of a basic evaluation matrix provide a wealth of information about the ends and means under consideration. They do not by themselves lead to a choice between alternatives. That choice must perforce rest on value judgements of the worth of one kind of outcome against another, for example, the worth of present economy in the utilisation of resources against flexibility to accommodate as yet unforeseen changes, the worth of benefiting one group in the community at the expense of another, the worth of achieving one objective while sacrificing another. Because such choices are not simple and do not emerge unequivocally from the facts, the act of choice and decision on policy in planning must be a political task. But as a basis for that political choice some kind of decision rule is helpful as a way of reducing the variety of the information which the matrix manipulations provide.

Two basic kinds of decision rule can be applied: an optimising rule and a satisficing rule.[23] Optimising seeks to choose the best alternative. To that end it prefers to regard ends as discriminatory objectives rather than constraints, it seeks to establish explicit relative priorities between objectives and thereby to derive an overall single criterion or objective function against which all alternatives can be measured. Satisficing seeks to choose an alternative that is good enough, or satisfactory, on the grounds that the absolute best can rarely be unambiguously identified. To that end it defines satisfactory performance levels for each objective, effectively turning objectives into constraints, and chooses the alternative which meets all those levels.

These kinds of decision rule can be applied in a variety of different ways to mixed matrices in planning evaluation to provide a basis for political choice. Three examples are a modified cost–benefit analysis approach, a ranking approach and a pure satisficing approach:

(i) The modified cost–benefit analysis approach would aggregate the monetary measures in the matrix, probably discounting their future to present day worth, and then calculate cost–benefit ratios or some such measure and draw a conclusion on preference; it would then consider whether the remaining measures, the so-called intangibles, outweigh the conclusions reached, possibly assisted by calculating the exchange rates between intangibles and monetary measures which would be implied by altering the initial order of preference.

(ii) The ranking approach would convert the diverse measures in the matrix, both monetary and non-monetary, into rank scores and aggregate them, with or without weighting by objectives, to give overall performance scores.

(iii) The pure satisficing approach would define target performance levels for each benefit measure, define overall or sectoral resource constraints, define acceptable distributional effects, for example, that no group should be worse off in the future than presently, and acceptable degrees of flexibility or robustness; it would then select the alternative which meets those constraints, and if there are more than one then some constraints could be increased.

All three of these approaches, and other similar versions of the basic optimising or satisficing decision rules, are directed towards the same end: providing a basis for political choice. Where they differ is in the form in which they require that political choice to be exercised. For some the choice lies in the selection of priorities, for others it lies in the choice of weights for objectives, and for yet others it lies in the determination of target performance levels. In none of them can political value judgements be disguised as technical fact finding. But through them, in their various ways, both technics and politics can be brought to bear on the act of choice which lies at the culmination of the evaluation essential to policy making.

ANALYSIS

Evaluation represents the central stand of decision and choice in policy making. But choices, to be rational, must be based on understanding. What must be understood are the change processes in the environment system with which planning is concerned—that is, changes in activities and their call on land resources. It is the task of the analytical strand in policy making to provide that understanding and feed it into evaluation. It does this by drawing on the information stored in the authority's information system. The process of policy review thus provides the link, shown in Fig. 10.3

* See Chapter 3.

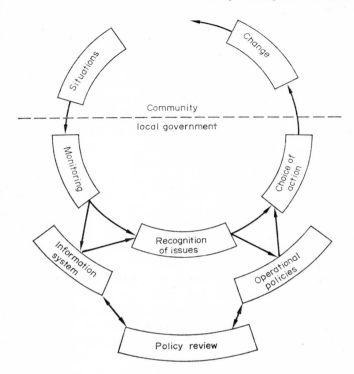

Fɪɢ. 10.3. Policy review and the action cycle.

between the authority's operational policies and its information system
Analysis can proceed through several levels of understanding—through
classification of data, to pattern building and correlation, and on to hypoth-
esising causal relationships. But at any level the particular classifications,
correlations or causal hypotheses do not arise directly from the data. They
are inevitably influenced by the authority's value system and yet they are
contributing to a plan review process undertaken in part to reconsider those
values as they are expressed in objectives and policies. There is then in
analysis always the problem of limiting the constraints on thought which
particular ways of organising and analysing data provide and of opening up
the possibilities of new analytical perceptions.

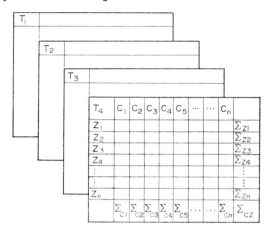

F<small>IG</small>. 10.4. Schematic system description.

Adequate system descriptions are a necessary start to analysis. These system descriptions exist in the local authority's information system which comprises the totality of its knowledge about the characteristics of the community environment and which is continually being supplemented with new data. The contents of that information system differ in their range of information, their level of detail and their periodicity. But notwithstanding this, each item in the system is classifiable by three dimensions of kind, location and time: for example, the population in an enumeration district at 1971. By extension a complete system description can be conceived as a series of files relating to variable kinds, locations or times.[24] Clearly the number of kinds, locations or times is potentially enormous, and in practice aggregation is a universal characteristic of system descriptions—locations are grouped into zones, kinds of variable into categories and times into time periods. Figure 10.4 illustrates such a system description in terms of zones $(Z_1, Z_2, Z_3, \text{etc.})$, categories $(C_1, C_2, C_3, \text{etc.})$ and time periods $(T_1, T_2, T_3, \text{etc.})$. From this simple presentation it is apparent that the system description has a capacity for summarising items in a number of ways which are useful in analysis. The row totals represent comprehensive descriptions of zonal characteristics at one point in time. The column totals represent the descriptions of spatial patterns of single variable categories at one point in time. The

grand total of both rows and columns represents a comprehensive description of the system as a whole at one point in time. Equally changes through
time in one variable category in one zone, in one variable across all zones, or
in the total system can be described.

But good system descriptions will by themselves be of limited value for
policy making. To facilitate understanding it is necessary to go beyond
system descriptions to the identification of relationships underlying the
operation of the environment system. This means proceeding by way of
correlations between variables to theories of cause and effect relating
variables. Correlations indicate patterns of association between one variable
and another and thereby provide a step beyond classification in analysing

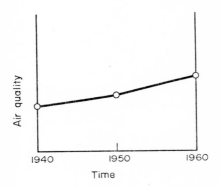

Fig. 10.5. Time period correlation or trend.

systems. Correlations indicate that some kind of relationship exists between
two variables. Such correlations can appear in any of the dimensions of the
system descriptions: between change in one time period and the next as, for
example, in the persistence of a trend in a variable through both periods
(Fig. 10.5); between two variables over a succession of zones such as, for
example, in relating incomes and length of journey to work (Fig. 10.6); and
interzonal relationships across different variables, for example, the correlation between density gradients and rent levels radial to city centres (Fig.
10.7). Such correlations can be displayed in graphical or tabular or map
form. They may or may not be measured statistically to put a precise value

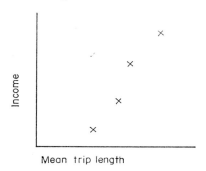

FIG. 10.6. Category correlation.

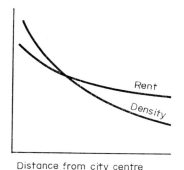

FIG. 10.7. Spatial correlation.

on the strengths of the relationship and to indicate the probability that it might have occurred by chance.[25]

To proceed through classification to pattern recognition and correlation may assist a presentation of present relationships and trends. In particular it provides a factual basis for the identification of classes of present and future problems and opportunities, particularly those which are persisting, either increasing or decreasing in intensity, and those which are taking closely linked, multiple forms. In this way the analytical work assists the redefinition of ends, both of objectives and constraints. At the same time classification and correlation analysis can be used to achieve that disaggregation within the policy space which is an essential prerequisite of the definition of mean through policy innovation: capital resource analysis, land potential analysis and social area analysis are all essentially classification and correlation techniques. But these represent the limits of the contribution of these kinds of analysis to policy making. To contribute further, through the prediction of outcomes for alternative policies, analysis must proceed from correlations to considerations of causality.

To interpret correlations and patterns of associations between variables in causal terms necessitates theory.[26] The theories needed concern the way activity systems and their claims on capital, land and human resources function. It might be observed that correlations exist between the condition of housing stock and the income of its residents; it requires theory, however, albeit of the simplest kind, to suggest that it is the latter which is influencing the former rather than vice versa. Only with the assistance of theory is it possible in this way to distinguish among correlated variables between dependent and independent variables, and thereby to express the relationships between variables as functional relationships in which changes in the dependent variable are functions of changes in the independent variable. The theory applied to the explanation of such functional relationships can be simple or complex: for example, the above relationship between housing conditions and household income could involve further consideration of household budgets, availability of capital, household structure, attitudes to tenure, landlord characteristics, location and local environmental quality. With the help of theories of causality it becomes possible to build models as simplified representations of these functional relationships between variables.[27] Such models may be expressed verbally, mathematically or iconically. Because they rest upon theories of causality, because they simplify complex relationships and, more in the case of mathematical models, because they can be manipulated with relative ease, models are operationally useful as techniques for predicting changes in system variables.

Activity systems interact closely in one functioning whole so that changes in one element spark off changes in other elements in continuous chain reactions. In principle it is impossible to predict change in one element without regard to how all other elements might be affected, and only a comprehensive model of total activity systems could achieve this. This is neither a practical possibility, given the present level of understanding, state of theory and availability of data, nor were it practicable would it be likely to be operationally useful since to be manageable it would perforce have to be highly aggregated. Instead partial models of those subsystems of relevance to the issues of concern to urban planning—subsystems of activities, land uses and transport systems, building stocks and environmental qualities —have greater operational value. These have regard to the interactions with other subsystems and can be linked together in a looser, less rigorous, comprehensive framework. Examples of some currently operational models are the landscape evaluation scales through which the impact of developmental changes on the character of landscapes can be assessed,[28] economic base models of employment growth and decline,[29] models of how density patterns and gradients change;[30] other examples are housing stock models through which changes in the composition and condition of the housing stock can be traced,[31] models of noise generation and attenuation,[32] activity allocation models of the locational pattern of land uses[33] and transport models of the travel demand and traffic flows they generate[34] and models of sewage discharge and the capacity of sewerage systems to accommodate them.[35] Some of these models have been made operational in mathematical terms, some only in verbal or iconic terms. In any of these forms, their value is as a basis for predicting the outcome of alternative policies under consideration in policy review.

They can do this because the dependent variables in the relationships they express are the variables which measure the outcomes relating to objectives which are of interest in evaluation, and because among the independent variables are variables which define the alternative policies alongside other variables with values determined quite outside planning policy and which are taken in the model as assumptions. It is through the explicit variation among the alternatives of the values for the policy variables that the model can predict the differing outcomes of those alternatives in terms of the dependent variables—predictions of consequential changes in traffic flows, landscape character, housing stock condition, noise levels and so on. Moreover, it is through explicit variation in the assumptions about the values of those independent variables determined outside planning policy, together with variations of the weights attached to objectives, that sensitivity analysis of the evaluation matrix to test alternatives against uncertainty can be undertaken. In these ways models have important contributions to make to policy making and review.

These analytical techniques of classification, correlation and modelling need a basic framework in which they can be handled in policy review. The three-dimensional nature of the items in system descriptions suggests a three-dimensional basis for such a framework, comprising locations, variables and times. Each of these can be aggregated or disaggregated for different kinds of analysis: the locations into zones and districts, the variables into topics, times into short-, medium- and long-term periods. Any of the classification, correlation or modelling analyses can focus on any of these dimensions—on trends through time, on patterns through space or on interrelated variables in time or space. The choice will depend basically on the kind of policy under review. Some may best be served by static or cross-sectional analyses of relationship at one point in time, others may require analyses of past change and prospective future change in one topic over time, yet others may need to focus on the totality of change in one area. The analytical techniques of classification, correlation and modelling, integrated within an overall framework, can contribute to all these kinds of policy review in helping to define classes of problems and opportunities, to identify the possibilities for policy alternatives and to predict the outcomes of those alternatives in terms which assist evaluation and choice.

CONSULTATION

Just as evaluation needs the support of analysis in reaching decisions on preferred policies, those policies, if they are to be effectively pursued, need to have demonstrably wide support among consumers, operators and developers in the community. Consultation in policy making and review embraces those processes by which support is sought for new policies under consideration. In policy review for planning it embraces three distinct but related kinds of interaction between the government and the community—consultation proper, participation and objection—each of which has developed somewhat separately. Consultation proper, comprising the exchange of information and advice mostly between public authorities about their mutual interests, objectives and intentions, is a recurrent aspect of all public administration. Participation, meaning the extension to all individuals and groups in the community of opportunities to have access to policy making processes and to influence possible policy at an early stage of its development, has recently become institutionalised in planning, but is essentially a reflection of changes in the relationship between the community and its government of relevance wider than the field of planning policy alone.[36] In contrast the procedures for making objections to policy statements put forward for approval or adoption have been long institutionalised in planning and derive directly from the concerns of planning, in that planning frequently affects directly proprietary rights over the use and ownership of land.

Consultation proper is desirable on three grounds. Firstly, consultation is needed with those public authorities, usually higher levels of government, possessing superior authority to local government such that their objectives and policies must be taken as a context in which particular policy making and review are being undertaken. For a structure plan this might mean consultation with a variety of agencies responsible for national and regional policies;[37] for a programme it would almost certainly mean consultation with the central government department exercising regulatory powers in that field; for a local plan prepared by a district it will mean pre-eminently consultation with the county structure plan authority.[38] Consultation of this kind will be eased where explicit policy statements are available which can be taken as definitive contexts—for example, a published and approved regional strategy. This will rarely be the case: such policy statements will either not exist, instead of which policy must be interpreted from executive decisions, or will be in need of updating, particularly significant for population and employment contexts, or will be expressed in such general terms that the specific local application of the policy is not clear. Clarification of context is necessary in all such cases.

Secondly, consultation is needed with subordinate, neighbouring or independent public authorities whose executive decisions and actions, sometimes subject to some degree of influence or regulation by the policy making authority, will be putting policies into effect.[39] Such are district authorities, neighbouring local authorities, independent authorities like water authorities or health authorities, statutory undertakers and some other public bodies. The local authority can seek to reflect the intentions of these bodies in their policies so that some degree of consistency in collective public policy exists.

Thirdly, consultation proper may be extended to interest groups within the community, like chambers of commerce, professional groups or amenity societies, which have established themselves as authoritative or representative within the community and whose experience and views the local authority is anxious to draw upon or whose agreement to their policy the local

thority is anxious to secure. All three kinds of consultation share a
mmon mode: they take the form of negotiation, usually in private, carried
t through the exchange of documents, reports and observations upon
ports, though sometimes supplemented by or even supplanted by joint
mmittees or working parties. They will normally be pursued until some
nsensus of view on desired policy is agreed.

Participation is a very different kind of activity.[40] Its intention is to
sure through publicity that the individuals in the community understand
e policy proposals and the reasoning in which they are based, to seek their
ews upon them and consider whether in the light of these to amend or to
alise that policy. It is therefore operating at a more fundamental level than
nsultation proper: both in being directed at the community at large and
being concerned not just to establish consistency of viewpoint and inten-
on but to establish basic values held by the community. It is essentially a
litical rather than an administrative activity. Where policy is expressed in
ructure plans and local plans then there is a statutory obligation for public
articipation, requiring publicity for the report of survey and publicity for
raft policies, and providing rights to individuals to make representations
pon them and have those representations considered, all of this to be
videnced to the Secretary of State for the Environment.[41] But even out-
de the development plan, participation is becoming an essential part of
nsultation procedures for policy making and review in planning.

If participation is to contribute effectively to evaluation and choice in
olicy making then it needs to possess a number of characteristics: it must
e representative, comprehensible and responsive.[42] Publicity should be
irected to and response sought from as wide a cross section of the commu-
ity as possible. Some organised groups may be able to respond to informa-
on presented in standard technical reports; some groups or individuals may
e reached through public meetings. But other modes—for example, films,
iscussion groups, attitude surveys, behavioural surveys, games—may need
xploiting to be sure that the participation experience is representative. The
istinction between the broad, strategic issues of the structure plan and the
ore precise, sometimes site or area or group specific issues of the local plans
nd programmes is important here: more indirect modes, like surveys, group
iscussions and games, may be more effective means of eliciting responses
n the former.[43]

Beyond representativeness in coverage the information made available in

participation needs to be comprehensible, likely to be understood by th
layman without recourse to expert advice. Language will be important an
the more recondite mathematical or iconic work in policy review will nee
translating into verbal terms, and everyday verbal terms at that, for partici
pation purposes. Additionally the perspective from which issues and polici
are presented can enhance their comprehensibility in two ways: firstly, b
expressing new policies as increases or decreases of some characteristic c
consumers' present experiences, such as travel times, air quality or choice c
housing; secondly, by expressing policies in the most tangible, concret
terms of what will happen as a consequence on the ground, in particula
subareas—for this reason a subarea presentation of the structure plan'
strategic policy is useful and the local plan is a more satisfactory vehicle fo
participation on tactical policy than the programme. In addition to languag
and choice of perspective, comprehensibility may be increased through
public presentation of the evaluation process central to policy makin
through which the draft policy has been derived, and, in particular, the basi
of the preference among the alternatives considered.

Participation is a two-way process. Just as important as widespread an
comprehensible publicity is the provision of channels by which representa
tions by individuals or groups within the community can reach the authority
And additionally there must be a willingness on the part of the authority t
respond to representations by considering them fully and giving to th
public and to the Secretary of State, where appropriate, their reasons fo
accepting or rejecting them. If the local authority is seen to be responsive t
participation, then the significance of objection, the third kind of interactio
between the authority and the community in policy making may be dimin
ished in importance.

Rights of objection exist in relation to proposed development plan polic
statements and also in relation to some other kinds of policy statement.[44
The distinction between objections and representations is two-fold. Objec
tions are to be made when the policy statement has been finalised and, in th
case of a structure plan, submitted to the Secretary of State for approval or
in the case of a local plan, is awaiting adoption, rather than at the earlier draf
policy stages. Further, objections commonly relate, by experience if not b
statute, to policies which will fairly directly and injuriously affect the interes
of the objector, whereas representations may be supporting or critical o
proposed policies on both interested or disinterested grounds.

Where objections are made, some procedure for considering these in ublic must follow. The form of this diverges between structure and local ans. For a local plan the consideration will normally be in the form of a cal public inquiry in which an inspector appointed by the Secretary of ate will hear the case presented by objectors and the case of the local anning authority regarding those objections, and will subsequently pre- re a report for the local authority.[45] They must consider his report, cide what action to take on each of its recommendations and publish their nclusions together with the report. Provided the Secretary of State has t exercised his power to call in the local plan for his approval, the local thority will then after a short period of time adopt the local plan as the licy statement.

For structure plans with their broader, strategic policies with a lesser rect impact on individual interests the procedures are different. To start ith the plan must be submitted for approval by the Secretary of State. But, yond that, there is no obligation on the Secretary of State to afford a right be heard to all objectors in any procedure for public consideration of the oposed policies. Rather than a public local inquiry there will be an amination in public of selected matters which the Secretary of State has fined as significant for his consideration of the plan.[46] To this end the cretary of State will define a set of issues on which the examination is to cus and invite selected persons, from among objectors or others, to join e local authority in a public debate of these issues before a panel appointed y him. The panel will report their conclusions to the Secretary of State who ill consider them, along with the objections earlier received, before pub- shing his decision on the plan together with the report of the panel.[47]

OLICY MAKING PROCESSES

These three strands of analysis, evaluation and consultation must be uitted together into a policy making process that moves systematically wards the taking of policy decisions and their expression in structure ans, local plans or programmes. The kinds of issue with which each kind f policy statement typically deals and the statutory and non-statutory con- entions governing their precise form, content and procedures must be an fluence on the form of policy making process appropriate to particular rcumstances. But in all circumstances analytical, evaluative and consulta- ve tasks will be inescapable components of policy making.

Furthermore, there are some basic principles appropriate to most circum
stances and by which these tasks may be most effectively integrated into
policy making process. Firstly, it is desirable to regard evaluation as th
basic strand of work into which analysis and consultation feed. The sequenc
of evaluative tasks—the definition of objectives and constraints, policy inn
vation, the measurement of outcomes, the manipulation of the matrice
their interpretation, the application of decision rules and the establishmer
of preferences—provide a basic process around which other work can b
structured. It is these evaluative tasks which lead directly to policy choice
Analysis, the understanding of relevant facts, and consultation, the valid
tion of relevant values, have importance only in relation to these choice
Effort on analytical and consultative tasks should be restricted, provide
that statutory obligations are satisfied where they exist, to what is neede
to inform evaluation.

Secondly, existing policies should be taken as a starting point so that th
process is essentially one of policy review rather than policy making. Fc
this there are a number of justifications. There should be an initial presump
tion in favour of continuity in policy simply because any change in polic
causes disruption and produces disbenefits: it must be demonstrated tha
the net benefits of new policies justify the discontinuity. Further a thorough
going assessment of present policies and their consequences provides a
insight into both ends and means: to avoid making such an assessment is t
fail to learn from past successes or failures. Present policies can also provid
a baseline for comparison of the costs and benefits of alternatives in term
that indicate whether new policy directions would yield better or wors
results than those familiar in present experience.

Thirdly, the policy review process should proceed incrementally in it
consideration of the future. It should look most immediately at wher
present policy commitments will lead in the short term, what problems an
opportunities will exist then, what ends and means seem appropriate. Onl
then should it proceed to a consideration of the medium and the long ter
which will be more or less uncertain.

In accordance with these principles policy making will always be a highl
evaluative, time related, reviewing kind of process. Nevertheless, th
emphasis on particular tasks will vary between policy making for structur
plans, programmes and local plans. In evaluation there will be an emphas
on resource utilisation in the preparation of programmes, there will be a

emphasis on distributional effects whenever participation is a required or desired component of policy making, there will be an emphasis on the response of alternatives to uncertainty in the long-term policies of structure plans. In consultation the relative minimum emphases on consultation proper, participation and rights of objection will be determined by statutory requirements but beyond that the precise way in which these tasks are approached will differ. Public participation on the broader, strategic policies of structure plans must be tackled differently from participation on the more detailed, site specific proposals of local plans; equally the clearer resource implications of programmes will make them a better basis for certain kinds of consultation on detailed proposals than local plans. Finally the precise focus of analysis must vary between circumstances. Outer bounds must always be defined to delimit the system under analysis and to simplify the interactions with external influences. But these limits, whether of location or time or kind of variable, can be wider or narrower in particular policy making circumstances. They should be widest in structure plan making concerned with subregions, long-term futures and a comprehensive range of policy fields. In comparison, and by definition, analysis for local plan making will be more restricted areally, analysis for programme making will be more restricted in range, though both might be more restricted also in the other dimensions where the needs of evaluation indicate specific emphases in analysis.

Underlying these variations in approach is a more fundamental question of how corporate an activity policy review should be. The traditional concern of urban planning with policy and policy making is being increasingly complemented by an increasing interest in explicit statements of policy by local authorities in other spheres of public affairs, while at the same time there is an increasing recognition of the interrelation of many environmental, social and economic issues. Where these developments proceed within the context of more corporately managed local authorities there can be foreseen the emergence of a corporate policy making and review function within the local government system. This seems likely to affect particularly the strategic policy making for the structure plan such that in time a policy review process for the structure plan might not exist independently of a strategic policy review process for the authority as a whole, which finds expression of its chosen policy partly in the structure plan, partly in other policy statements covering economic and social affairs. Programme making may be a less corporate activity provided there is adherence to the constraining context of strategic policy. But local plans which, like structure plans, integrate policy across a range of topics, might be the product of a corporate, albeit localised process of policy review focused on the issues, either environmental or economic or social, arising in parts of the local authority area.

Policy review benefits from a corporate approach. Even where executive decision making is relatively fragmented in various decision fields, it is desirable that policy should be expressed in a more integrated way and that policy making should range more broadly still: there should be fewer policy fields than executive fields and even fewer policy making processes than policy fields. Where authorities are structured with strong, vertically organised departments, with each department embracing all functions from executive action through to the most strategic policy making, then policy making will suffer from the consequentially narrow definition of the policy space. Only by breaking down compartmentalised organisation and thinking can the bounds of the policy space be set wide enough to provide an opportunity for effective policy making and review.

Whether that opportunity is grasped or not depends largely on the skills, chiefly professional but also political, which are brought to bear on it. Policy review in planning requires many skills—professionally there are roles for political scientists, architects, physical planners, economists, engineers, sociologists, statisticians, systems analysts and others. But two particular skills, neither of them the preserve of particular professions, are essential: skill in innovation and skill in interpretation.

Innovation in planning policy means no more than the process by which new possibilities for ends and means of policy come into consideration. It is a counterprocess to the inevitable inertia through which established perspectives and policies remain unchallenged long past their period of usefulness. Innovative skills combine therefore a critical ability with an imaginative ability, a negative with a positive side. Both of these are assisted by an ability to take a broad view, to see traditionally unrelated facts or policies in juxtaposition. Such innovative skill is likely to be a skill personal to particular individuals, but it may also be stimulated within a situation in which the government system as a whole accepts the necessity of learning, of continually questioning its own ends and means;[48] it may also be encouraged where corporate rather than departmental attitudes towards policy prevail, such that the total policy space of the authority is less compartmentalised

d all the powers, moneys, skills, manpower and property available to the
thority are potentially available for application in finding new policies for
gulating any of the kinds of community change to which the authority
shes to respond.

Skills in interpretation are needed to translate the languages used in the
ferent strands and stages of the policy making process: it may mean the
erpretation of the output of mathematical models in terms which are
lpful to politicians, it may mean interpreting the experience of public
rticipation exercises to help with evaluation, it may mean interpreting the
licy implicit in a number of past decisions in order to elucidate constraints
r policy alternatives. The process of policy making itself must proceed,
ternally at least, with its own set of consistent linguistic conventions. The
ill of relating these to the varying languages around policy making is one
which the success of policy making and in due course of policy itself is
ry dependent.

Further Reading

AUTHORS customarily recommend for further reading what was their prior readin.
What follows therefore is a brief note on writings which originated or inspired sor
of the ideas in the preceding chapters. It covers politics, public administratio.
policy and policy making, both generally and specifically related to urban plannin.

J. D. B. Miller's *The Nature of Politics* (Duckworth, London, 1972; Pengui.
Harmondsworth, 1965) deals with a lot of basic issues relevant to policy in urb.
planning including pluralism, the concept of the public interest and the impact.
ideas and ideologies. It also has a good list of further reading in political scienc.
Peter Self's *Administrative Theories and Politics* (Allen & Unwin, London, 197.
contains a wealth of perceptive observations on the nature of administrati.
organisation and behaviour.

J. A. G. Griffith's *Central Departments and Local Authorities* (Allen & Unwin.
London, 1966) is still the best introduction to the influence of central governme.
on local policy and executive action and has a section on planning. On local gover.
ment itself there has been a flood of writing in the last few years, some of it bas.
on general analyses and some of it based on direct observation. Of the former To.
Eddison's *Local Government: Management and Corporate Planning* (Leonard Hi.
Aylesbury, 1973) is both informative and thought-provoking, and of the latt.
J. K. Friend and W. N. Jessop's *Local Government and Strategic Choice* (Tavistoc.
London, 1969) is the most original, particularly in its view of the local authority.
a controller of societal change.

The substance of environmental affairs has been worked over recently by a ma.
of writing, much of it by prophets of ecological disaster. Lynton Caldwell.
Environment: A Challenge to Modern Society (Doubleday, New York, 1971), whi.
sharing much of their pessimism, does at least address itself to the basic scientifi.
ethical and administrative problems to be resolved in any redirection of enviror.
mental policy. Peter Gresswell's *Environment: An Alphabetical Handbook* (Joh.
Murray, London, 1971) is an invaluable guide to issues, powers, procedures an.
institutions in British environmental affairs and D. A. Bigham's *The Law an.
Administration Relating to the Protection of the Environment* (Oyez, London, 197.
usefully covers pollution, transport and housing as well as planning, conservatio.
and the countryside. Melvin Webber's essay "Permissive Planning" (*Town Plannin.
Review*, **40**, 1 (1969); also available as Working Paper 18, Centre for Environment.
Studies, London, 1968) still stands as a lone attempt to apply some basic rational.
of public policy to urban planning.

The nature of policy and the process of policy making are much illuminated b.

Sir Geoffrey Vickers' *The Art of Judgement* (Chapman & Hall, London, 1965) particularly through his distinctions between policy and execution, his view of policy as norms and his emphasis on the interrelations of fact and value. He acknowledges a debt to H. A. Simon whose *Administrative Behaviour* (Macmillan, New York, 2nd ed. 1957) is still worth reading for his exposition of rationality in decision making although his "Theories of Decision Making in Economics and Behavioural Science" (in ed. G. P. E. Clarkson, *Managerial Economics*, Penguin, Harmondsworth, 1968) summarises his thinking. Donald Schon's *Beyond the Stable State* (Temple Smith, London, 1971), particularly Chapter 5 on "Government as a Learning System", has interesting things to say about the evolution of ideas in public policy.

Of writing on policy making in planning so much presents a view of a process which is entirely technical in content and which is totally divorced from executive decisions. J. Brian McLoughlin's *Urban and Regional Planning* (Faber & Faber, London, 1969) is a good summary account of the developing systems approach to the analytical tasks of policy making. Colin Lee's *Models in Planning* (Pergamon, Oxford, 1973) introduces that particular analytical tool. The evaluative tasks are covered well in the Department of the Environment's Structure Plans Notes 7/72 *Evaluating Alternatives in Structure Plan Making* and 8/72 *The Use of Evaluation Matrices for Structure Plans* (Department of the Environment, London, 1972). The political and administrative aspects of policy making in urban planning have not been well written about in general terms, although there is a flourishing literature of case studies of urban decision making awaiting the attention of theoreticians.

References

Introduction

1. FRIEDMANN, JOHN (1969) Notes on societal action, *Journal of the American Institute of Planners*, **35**, 5.
2. See, for example, MCLOUGHLIN, J. BRIAN (1969) *Urban and Regional Planning, A Systems Approach*, Faber, London; and CHADWICK, GEORGE (1971) *A Systems View of Planning*, Pergamon, Oxford.
3. This trend is discussed in VICKERS, Sir GEOFFREY (1965) *The Art of Judgement*, Methuen, London, Chap. 10; and SELF, PETER (1972) The State versus man, in ROBSON, WILLIAM A. (ed.) *Man and the Social Sciences*, Allen & Unwin.
4. BENEVOLO, LEONARDO (1967) *The Origins of Modern Town Planning*, Routledge, London; ASHWORTH, W. (1954) *The Genesis of Modern British Town Planning*, Routledge, London.
5. WEBBER, MELVIN M. (1968) *Beyond the Industrial Age and Permissive Planning*, Working Paper 18, Centre for Environmental Studies, London. Webber identifies nine rationales but some have been grouped together here.
6. MCLOUGHLIN, J. B. (1965) Notes on the nature of physical change, *Journal of the Town Planning Institute*, **51**, 10.
7. SELF, PETER (1972) Planning and politics, *Town and Country Planning*, **40**, 9.
8. See WEBBER (1968) *op. cit.*, on the influence of the civil engineering style on city planning.
9. MILLER, J. D. B. (1962) *The Nature of Politics*, Duckworth, London, Chap. 1,
10. SIMON, H. A. (1957 2nd ed.) *Administrative Behaviour*, Macmillan, New York. Chap. 3.
11. VICKERS (1965) *op. cit.*, Chap. 2.

Chapter 1

1. MARSHALL, ALFRED (8th ed. 1949) *Principles of Economics*, Macmillan, London, Book IV, Chap. 1.
2. BURNS, TOM (1968) Urban styles of life, in *The Future of the City Region*, S.S.R.C./C.E.S. Joint Conference Papers, Vol. 2, Working Paper 6, Centre for Environmental Studies, London.
3. HALSEY, A. H. (Ed.) (1972) *Trends in British Society Since 1960*, Macmillan, London, gives an interesting historical account; and WILLMOTT, PETER (1973) Some social trends, in CULLINGWORTH, J. B. (ed.) *Problems of an Urban Society*, Vol. III, Allen & Unwin, London, considers likely future changes.
4. For a brief account of present statistical sources on income and expenditure see CENTRAL STATISTICAL OFFICE (1971) *Social Trends No. 2*, H.M.S.O., London, p. 69.
5. GENERAL REGISTER OFFICE (1971) *Classification of Occupations 1970*, H.M.S.O., London. See also HALL, C. B. and SMITH, R. A. (1968) Socio-economic patterns of England and Wales, *Urban Studies*, **5**, 1.

6. SOUTH EAST JOINT PLANNING TEAM (1971) *Strategic Plan for the South East, Studies Vol. 2, Social and Environment Aspects*, H.M.S.O., London, Chap. 2.
7. See, for example, in England WILLMOTT, PETER (1963) *The Evolution of a Community*, Routledge, London; and in the United States GANS, HERBERT J. (1967) *The Levittowners*, Allen Lane, London.
8. LICHFIELD, NATHANIEL (1956) Economics of planned development, *Estates Gazette*, London, Chap. 8.
9. See CHAPIN, F. STUART, Jr. (1965) *Urban Land Use Planning*, University of Illinois Press, Urbana, Chap. 6.
10. BEST, ROBIN H. and CHAMPION, A. G. (1969) *Regional Conversion of Agricultural Land to Urban Use in England and Wales 1945–67*, University Working Paper No. 3, Centre for Environmental Studies, London.
11. STONE, P. A. (1964) Urban development and national resources, *Urban Studies*, **1**, 2.
12. BEST, ROBIN H. (1968) Competition for land between rural and urban uses, in *Land Uses and Resources: Studies in Applied Geography*, Institute of British Geographers, London.
13. MCLOUGHLIN (1969) *op. cit.*, Chap. 1.
14. For an introduction to systems concepts see MCLOUGHLIN, J. BRIAN and WEBSTER, JUDITH N. (1970) Cybernetic and general system approaches to urban, and regional research: a review of the literature, *Environment and Planning*, **2**.
15. MCLOUGHLIN (1965) *op. cit.*
16. For a discussion of the emergence and substance of environmental affairs see CALDWELL, LYNTON KEITH (1971) *Environment, A Challenge to Modern Society*. Doubleday, New York.

Chapter 2

1. ACKOFF, RUSSELL L. (1970) *A Concept of Corporate Planning*, Wiley–Interscience, New York, Chap. 2.
2. See TURVEY, RALPH (ed.) (1968) *Public Enterprise: Selected Readings*, Penguin, London.
3. See LICHFIELD, NATHANIEL (1956) *op. cit.*, Chap. 1; and LEAN, W. and GOODALL, B. (1966) Aspects of land economics *Estates Gazette*, London, Chap. 6.
4. KNOWLES, F. C. (1970) Financing urban renewal, in *Report of Proceedings, Town and Country Planning Summer School*, 1970, Town Planning Institute, London.
5. GALBRAITH, JOHN KENNETH (1967) *The New Industrial State*, Hamish Hamilton, London.
6. See DONNISON, D. V. (1970) Government and governed, *New Society*, 5 March; and STYLES, B. J. (1971) Public participation—a reconsideration, *Journal of the Town Planning Institute*, **57**, 4.
7. The *modus operandi* of local government has been the subject of a number of recent studies: BOADEN, NOEL (1971) *Urban Policy Making: Influences on County Boroughs in England and Wales*, Cambridge University Press, London; FRIEND, J. K. and JESSOP, W. N. (1969) *Local Government and Strategic Choice*, Tavistock, London; and STEWART, J. D. (1971) *Management in Local Government*, Charles Knight, London.

8. BURKE, TERENCE J. (1972) Effective local government, *Journal of the Royal Town Planning Institute*, **58**, 8.
9. For a comprehensive account of local authority environmental powers see GRESSWELL, PETER (1971) *Environment: an Alphabetical Handbook*, John Murray, London.
10. EVERSLEY, DAVID (1972) Rising costs and static incomes: some consequences of regional planning in London, *Urban Studies*, **9**, 3.
11. GRIFFITHS, J. A. G. (1966) *Central Departments and Local Authorities*, Allen & Unwin, London.

Chapter 3

1. This representation is derived in modified form from FRIEND and JESSOP (1969) *op. cit.*, Chap. 5.
2. FRIEND and JESSOP (1969) *op. cit.*, Chap. 7.
3. This section draws heavily on *General Information System for Planning* (1972). Report of Joint Local Authority, Scottish Development Department and Department of the Environment Study Team, H.M.S.O., London.
4. BAUER, RAYMOND A. (ed.) (1966) *Social Indicators*, M.I.T. Press, Boston; SHONFIELD, ANDREW and SHAW, STELLA (eds.) (1972) *Social Indicators and Social Policy*, Heinemann, London.
5. WEBBER, MELVIN M. (1965) The role of intelligence systems in urban systems planning, *Journal of the American Institute of Planners*, **31**, 11.
6. GRIFFITHS (1966) *op. cit.*, pp. 54–74.
7. Caravan Sites Act, 1968, Part II.
8. Housing Act, 1957, Part II.
9. National Parks and Access to the Countryside Act, 1949, Parts IV and V.
10. *Department of the Environment Circular 12/72, The Planning of the Undeveloped Coast*, H.M.S.O., London.
11. *Department of the Environment Circular 10/73, Planning and Noise*, H.M.S.O., London.
12. *Department of the Environment Circular 17/72, Out of Town Shops and Shopping Centres*, and Department of the Environment Development Control Policy Note (1972) *Out of Town Shops and Shopping Centres*, H.M.S.O., London.
13. *Department of the Environment Circular 86/72, Town and Country Planning (Amendment) Act 1972: Conservation*, H.M.S.O., London.
14. BOADEN (1971) *op. cit.*, Chap. 3.
15. DONNISON, D. V. (1972) Ideologies and policies, *Journal of Social Policy*, **1**, 2.
16. SCHON, DONALD A. (1971) *Beyond the Stable State*, Temple Smith, London, notes the importance of changes in the climate of opinion in public administration.
17. FRIEND and JESSOP (1969) *op. cit.*, p. 105.
18. Housing Act, 1969, Part II.
19. ETZIONI, AMITAI (1968) *The Active Society: a Theory of Societal and Political Processes*, Collier–Macmillan, London, p. 250.
20. FRIEND and JESSOP (1969) *op. cit.*, p. 105.
21. VICKERS (1965) *op. cit.*, p. 25.

Chapter 4

1. See VICKERS (1965) *op. cit.*, p. 31, for a fuller exposition of a norm setting rather than goal setting view of policy.

2. Vickers (1965) *op. cit.*, Chap. 1.
3. Webber (1968) *op. cit.*, criticises planning's over-reliance on simple two variable standards for the expression of policy.
4. Friend and Jessop (1969) *op. cit.*, p. 108.

Chapter 5

1. These are in fact the matters to which policy in structure and local plans are to relate in accordance with S.I. 1971 No. 1109, *Town and Country Planning (Structure and Local Plans) Regulations 1971*, H.M.S.O., London. But they illustrate the standard list of topics.
2. On geographers' approaches to defining areas see Haggett, Peter (1965) *Locational Analysis in Human Geography*, Edward Arnold, London, Chap. 9; and Grigg, David (1967) Regions, models and classes, in Chorley, Richard J. and Haggett, Peter (eds.) *Models in Geography*, Methuen, London.
3. These problems are well documented in Cmnd. 4040 (1969) *Royal Commission on Local Government in England 1966–1969, Volume I, Report*, H.M.S.O., London.
4. Massey, Doreen B. (1973) The basic:nonbasic categorisation in planning, *Regional Studies*, **7**, March.
5. Jones, Richard M. (1970) Local labour markets, the journey to work and government location policy, *Town Planning Review*, **41**, 2.
6. The distinction between strategy and tactics derives, of course, from military planning: see Wilson, Andrew (1970) *War Gaming*, Penguin, London. In its application to public policy it has been developed beyond the loosest kind of analogy by Etzioni (1968) *op. cit.*, Chap. 12.
7. The example is from Etzioni (1968) *op. cit.*
8. Ashby, W. R. (1964) *An Introduction to Cybernetics*, Methuen, London, Chap. 11.
9. Ackoff (1970) *op. cit.*, Chap. 1.
10. Schlesinger, James R. (1969) *Organisational Structures and Planning*, C.A.S. Reprint Papers, 1, H.M.S.O., London.

Chapter 6

1. For a fuller account see Heap, Desmond (1973, 6th ed.) *An Outline of Planning Law*, Sweet & Maxwell, London.
2. Town and Country Planning Act, 1962, Part II.
3. S.I. 1965 No. 1453, *Town and Country Planning (Development Plans) Regulations*.
4. *Ministry of Town and Country Planning, Circular 63/49, Report of the Survey*, H.M.S.O., London.
5. For a detailed account of these inadequacies see Ministry of Housing and Local Government, Ministry of Transport and Scottish Development Department (1965) *The Future of Development Plans, Report of the Planning Advisory Group*, H.M.S.O., London; and Cmnd. 3333, (1967) *Town and Country Planning*, H.M.S.O., London. They are well summarised in Department of the Environment (1973) *Greater London Development Plan, Report of the Panel of Inquiry, Vol. I, Report*, H.M.S.O., London, Chap. 2.
6. Model terms of reference are quoted in Leicester City Council and Leicestershire County Council (1969) *Leicester and Leicestershire Subregional*

Planning Study, Vol. I, Report and Recommendations, p. 5. See also COWLING
T. M. and STEELEY, G. C. (1973) *Subregional Planning Studies: an Evaluation*
Pergamon, Oxford.

7. *Ministry of Transport and Ministry of Housing Joint Circular 1/64, The Buchanan
Report: Traffic in Towns*, H.M.S.O., London; *Ministry of Transport Roads
Circular 8/65, Future Planning of Urban Classified Roads*, H.M.S.O., London.
Transportation studies as instruments of policy making are discussed in
SPENCE, R. (1968) Transportation studies: a critical assessment, *Proc. of the
Transportation Engineering Conference*, Institute of Civil Engineers, London,
in SOLESBURY, WILLIAM and TOWNSEND, ALAN (1970) Transportation studies
and British planning practice, *Town Planning Review*, **41**, 1; and in PLOWDEN,
STEPHEN (1972) *Towns Against Traffic*, Deutsch, London.

8. *Department of the Environment Circular 104/73, Local Transport Grants,*
H.M.S.O., London.

9. *Ministry of Transport Roads Circular 1/68, Traffic and Transport Plans,*
H.M.S.O., London.

10. MINISTRY OF HOUSING AND LOCAL GOVERNMENT AND MINISTRY OF TRANSPORT
(1962) *Planning Bulletin 1, Town Centres: Approach to Renewal*, H.M.S.O.,
London.

11. MINISTRY OF HOUSING AND LOCAL GOVERNMENT (1967) *Planning Bulletin 8,
Settlement in the Countryside: a Planning Method*, H.M.S.O., London.

12. Town and Country Planning Act, 1971, Part IV, s. 63.

13. Clean Air Act, 1956, Clean Air Act, 1968.

14. Civic Amenities Act, 1967, Part I; Town and Country Planning (Amendment)
Act, 1972, s. 10.

15. Housing Act, 1969, Part II.

16. For a fuller account see HEAP (1973) *op. cit.*

17. Town and Country Planning Act, 1971, Part II.

18. *Department of the Environment Circular 44/71, Memorandum on Part I of the
Town and Country Planning Act, 1968*, H.M.S.O., London, paras. 33 to 48.

19. Local Government Act, 1972, s. 183(2).

20. Town and Country Planning (Amendment) Act, 1972, s. 3.

21. S.I. 1971 No. 1109, *op. cit.*, Part IV; *Department of the Environment Circular
44/71* (1971) *Memorandum, op. cit.*, paras. 13–18; MINISTRY OF HOUSING AND
LOCAL GOVERNMENT (1970) *Development Plans, A Manual on Form and
Content*, H.M.S.O., London, Chaps. 3–6.

22. S.I. 1971 No. 1109, *op. cit.*, Part V; *Department of the Environment Circular
44/71, Memorandum, op. cit.*, paras. 19–25; MINISTRY OF HOUSING AND LOCAL
GOVERNMENT (1970) *op. cit.*, Chaps. 7–10.

23. *Ministry of Housing and Local Government Circular 66/68, Town and Country
Planning Act 1968, Town and Country Planning Act 1968 (Commencement No. 1)
Order 1968*, H.M.S.O., London.

24. *Department of the Environment Circular 44/71, Memorandum, op. cit.*, paras. 10,
98.

25. STEWARD, J. D. and EDDISON, TONY (1971) Structure planning and corporate
planning, *Journal of the Royal Town Planning Institute*, **57**, 8.

26. GREENWOOD, R., SMITH, A. D. and STEWART, J. D. (1971) *New Patterns of
Local Government Organisation*, Occasional Paper 5, Institute of Local Government Studies, University of Birmingham.

27. HACK, J. S. and PAILING, K. B. (1972) The development plan system and corporate planning, *Local Government Finance*, **76**, 12.
28. STEWART, J. D. (1972) Community and corporate planning in two tier local government, *Journal of Royal Town Planning Institute*, **58**, 8.

Chapter 7

1. A useful review of concepts is given in McLOUGHLIN, J. BRIAN and THORNLEY, JENNIFER (1972) *Some Problems in Structure Planning: a literature review*, Information Paper 27, Centre for Environmental Studies, London.
2. For a progress report see McLOUGHLIN, J. BRIAN (1973) Structure planning in Britain, *Journal of the Royal Town Planning Institute*, **59**, 3.
3. S.I. 1971 No. 1109, *op. cit.*
4. *Department of the Environment Circular 44/71, Memorandum, op. cit.*
5. MINISTRY OF HOUSING AND LOCAL GOVERNMENT (1970) *op. cit.*
6. See McLOUGHLIN (1973) *op. cit.*
7. GREATER LONDON COUNCIL (1969) *Greater London Development Plan*, G.L.C., London; DEPARTMENT OF THE ENVIRONMENT (1973) *Greater London Development Plan, Report of the Panel of Inquiry*, H.M.S.O., London.
8. These five functions are adapted from MINISTRY OF HOUSING AND LOCAL GOVERNMENT (1970) *op. cit.*, para. 3.10.
9. Like, for example, SOUTH EAST JOINT PLANNING TEAM (1971) *op. cit.*
10. Town and Country Planning Act, 1971, s. 7.
11. Town and Country Planning (Amendment) Act, 1972, s. 1.
12. *Department of the Environment Circular 44/71, Memorandum, op. cit.*, paras. 44–45; MINISTRY OF HOUSING AND LOCAL GOVERNMENT (1970) *op. cit.*, paras. 4.4–4.5.
13. MINISTRY OF HOUSING AND LOCAL GOVERNMENT (1970) *op. cit.*, para. 4.6.
14. Local Government Act, 1972, s. 183(2).
15. S.I. 1971 No. 1109, *op. cit.*, Regulation 8; *Department of the Environment Circular 44/71, Memorandum, op. cit.*, paras. 15–18.
16. Town and Country Planning Act, 1971, s. 7(5).
17. MINISTRY OF HOUSING AND LOCAL GOVERNMENT (1970) *op. cit.*, paras. 4.18–4.20.
18. Town and Country Planning Act, 1971, s. 7(3).
19. Town and Country Planning Act, 1971, s. 22.
20. *Department of the Environment Circular 44/71, Memorandum, op. cit.*, paras. 35–6.
21. S.I. 1971 No. 1109, *op. cit.*, schedule 1, Part I.
22. By virtue of Town and Country Planning Act, 1971, s. 23(1).
23. Town and Country Planning Act, 1971, s. 29(1).
24. *Department of the Environment Circular 44/71, Memorandum, op. cit.*, para. 30.
25. MINISTRY OF HOUSING AND LOCAL GOVERNMENT (1970) *op. cit.*, para. 1.7.
26. *Department of the Environment Circular 44/71, Memorandum, op. cit.*, para. 13.
27. MINISTRY OF HOUSING AND LOCAL GOVERNMENT (1970) *op. cit.*, para. 2.7.
28. See *Department of the Environment Circular 44/71, Memorandum, op. cit.*, para. 13; and DEPARTMENT OF THE ENVIRONMENT (1973) *op. cit.*, Chaps. 2 and 28.
29. MINISTRY OF HOUSING AND LOCAL GOVERNMENT (1970) *op. cit.*, paras. 4.14–4.16.
30. *Ibid.*, Chap. 5.

31. S.I. 1971 No. 1109, *op. cit.*, Regulation 12(2).
32. *Department of the Environment Circular 44/71, Memorandum, op. cit.*, para. 13.
33. MINISTRY OF HOUSING AND LOCAL GOVERNMENT (1970) *op. cit.*, 3.19.
34. *Ibid.*, para. 6.6.
35. See, for example, *Department of Health and Social Security Circular 35/72, Local Authority Social Services 10 Year Development Plans 1973–1983,* D.H.S.S., London.

Chapter 8

1. STEWART (1971) *op. cit.*, Chap. 9.
2. See GRESSWELL (1971) *op. cit.*
3. See McLOUGHLIN, J. (1972) *The Law Relating to Pollution*, Manchester University Press, Manchester, Chap. 6.
4. Town and Country Planning Act, 1971, Part III; Highways Act, 1959, Part III.
5. CLARKE, Sir RICHARD (1972) The number and size of government departments, *Political Quarterly*, **43**, April–June.
6. *Department of the Environment Circular 2/70, Capital Programmes*, H.M.S.O., London.
7. *Department of the Environment Circular 10/73, Planning and Noise*, H.M.S.O., London.
8. Local Government Act, 1972, Part I.
9. Water Act, 1973.
10. *Department of the Environment Circular 121/72, Local Government Act, 1972*, Appendix A.
11. STEWART (1971) *op. cit.*, Chap. 5.
12. MACMURRAY, TREVOR (1973) Housing processes and planning, *Journal of the Royal Town Planning Institute*, **59**, 2.
13. Housing Acts, 1957, 1961, 1964, 1971; Public Health Acts, 1936, 1961; Town and Country Planning Act, 1971.
14. DEPARTMENT OF THE ENVIRONMENT (1972) *Working Party on Local Authority/Private Enterprise Partnership Schemes, Report*, H.M.S.O., London.
15. Clean Air Acts, 1956, 1968; Public Health Act, 1936; Noise Abatement Act, 1960; Public Health (Recurring Nuisances) Act, 1969; Rivers (Prevention of Pollution) Acts, 1951, 1961; Clean Rivers (Estuaries and Tidal Waters) Act, 1960; Water Resources Act, 1963; Water Act, 1973; Civic Amenities Act, 1967; Deposit of Poisonous Wastes Act, 1972; Town and Country Planning Act, 1971. See also WILLIAMS, A. J. (1973) The role of the local planning authority in regard to waste and pollution, *Journal of Planning and Environmental Law*, January.
16. Highway Acts, 1959, 1971; Transport Acts, 1962, 1968; Town and Country Planning Act, 1971; Local Government Act, 1972; Land Compensation Act, 1972.
17. Cmnd. 5366 (1973) *Urban Transport Planning*, H.M.S.O., London.

Chapter 9

1. Town and Country Planning Act, 1971, Part II.
2. S.I. 1971 No. 1109, *op. cit.*
3. *Department of the Environment Circular 44/71, Memorandum, op. cit.*

4. MINISTRY OF HOUSING AND LOCAL GOVERNMENT (1970) *op. cit.*
5. Local Government Act, 1972, s. 183(2).
6. These three functions are adapted from MINISTRY OF HOUSING AND LOCAL GOVERNMENT (1970) *op. cit.*, para. 7.3.
7. Local Government Act, 1972, Schedule 16, para. 3(2).
8. *Department of the Environment Circular 44/71, Memorandum, op. cit.*, paras. 19–23; MINISTRY OF HOUSING AND LOCAL GOVERNMENT (1970), *op. cit.*, para. 7.2.
9. *Department of the Environment Circular 44/71, Memorandum, op. cit.*, paras. 95–97.
10. S.I. 1971 No. 1109, *op. cit.*, Schedule 2.
11. *Department of the Environment Circular 44/71, Memorandum, op. cit.*, para. 22.
12. WOODGATE, R. S. (1966) *Planning by Network: Project Planning and Control Using Network Techniques*, Business Publications, London.
13. S.I. 1971, No. 1109, *op. cit.*, Regulation 11.
14. For example, the provisions of the Local Authority Social Services Act, 1970, for area administration of social services.
15. Local Government Act, 1972, s. 195.
16. MINISTRY OF HOUSING AND LOCAL GOVERNMENT (1970) *op. cit.*, para. 8.17.

Chapter 10

1. SIMON (1957) *op. cit.*, p. 5.
2. See SIMON (1957) *op. cit.*, Chap. 4; MEYERSON, M. and BANFIELD, E. (1955) *Politics, Planning and the Public Interest*, Free Press, Glencoe; McLOUGHLIN (1969) *op. cit.*, Chap. 5; ETZIONI (1968) *op. cit.*, Chap. 11.
3. BOYCE, D. E. (1971) The metropolitan plan making process: its theory and practical complexities, in WILSON, A. G. (ed.) *London Papers in Regional Science 2*, Pion, London.
4. For a discussion of this and the counter view of "disjointed incrementalism" as an alternative paradigm of decision making see WEBBER (1965) *op. cit.*, and ETZIONI (1968) *op. cit.*, Chap. 11.
5. *Department of the Environment Circular 44/71, Memorandum, op. cit.*, para. 41.
6. SELF, PETER (1972) *Administrative Theories and Politics*, Allen & Unwin, London, Chap. 8.
7. WHITBREAD, MICHAEL (1972) *Evaluation in the Planning Process*, Working Paper 3, Planning Methodology Research Unit, University College, London; PERRATON, JEAN (1972) *Evaluation as Part of the Planning Process*, Working Paper 33, Centre for Land Use and Built Form Studies, Cambridge.
8. DEPARTMENT OF THE ENVIRONMENT (1972) *Structure Plans Note 8/72, The Use of Evaluation Matrices for Structure Plans*, Department of the Environment, London.
9. GUTCH, RICHARD M. (1972) *Goals and the Planning Process*, Oxford Working Papers in Planning Education and Research, no. 11, Oxford Polytechnic.
10. HARRIS, BRITTON (1967) The city of the future: the problem of optimal design, *Papers of the Regional Science Association*, **19**.
11. For a discussion of disaggregation in the design process see ALEXANDER, CHRISTOPHER (1966) *Notes on the Synthesis of Form*, Harvard University Press, Cambridge.
12. EDDISON, TONY (1973) *Local Government: Management and Corporate Planning*, Leonard Mill, Aylesbury, Chap. 4.

13. FORBES, JEAN (1969) A map analysis of potentially developable land, *Regional Studies*, **3**, 2.
14. PAHL, R. E. (1969) Whose city?, *New Society*, January 23.
15. For an introduction to the general literature on creativity see KOESTLER, ARTHUR (1964) *The Act of Creation*, Hutchinson, London.
16. VICKERS (1965) *op. cit.*, Chap. 6.
17. PEARCE, D. W. (1971) *Cost Benefit Analysis*, Macmillan, London, Chap. 6.
18. An impressive example of the development of performance measures is given by Coventry City Council (1971) *Coventry–Solihull–Warwickshire, A Strategy for the Subregion, Supplementary Report 4*; see also WHITBREAD, MICHAEL (1973) *Measurement in Evaluation*, Working Paper 6, Planning Methodology Research Unit, University College, London.
19. For example, the recommendation of the Urban Motorways Committee that environmental effects should enter highway evaluations: DEPARTMENT OF THE ENVIRONMENT (1972) *New Roads in Towns, Report of the Urban Motorways Committee*, H.M.S.O., London, para. 2.4.
20. DEPARTMENT OF THE ENVIRONMENT (1972) *Structure Plans Note 7/72, Evaluating Alternatives in Structure Plan Making*, Department of the Environment, London.
21. CHMARA, E. and LANGLEY, P. (1973) Evaluation matrices for structure plans, *P.T.R.C. Summer Annual Meeting, Proceedings*, P.T.R.C., London.
22. PEARCE, D. W. (1971) *op. cit.*, Chap. 5.
23. "Optimising is the science of the ultimate; satisficing is the art of the feasible", EILON, SAMUEL (1972) Goals and constraints in decision making, *OR Quarterly*, **23**, 1; see also ACKOFF (1970) *op. cit.*, Chap. 1.
24. General Information System for Planning (1972), *op. cit.*, Appendix B.
25. MORONEY, M. J. (1956 3rd ed.) *Facts from Figures*, Penguin, London, Chap. 15.
26. HARRIS, BRITTON (1966) The uses of theory in the simulation of urban phenomena, *Journal of the American Institute of Planners*, **32**, 5.
27. MASSER, IAN (1972) *Analytical Models for Urban and Regional Planning*, David and Charles, Newton Abbot; LEE, COLIN (1973) *Models in Planning*, Pergamon, Oxford.
28. LANDSCAPE RESEARCH GROUP (1967) *Methods of Landscape Analysis*, Symposium Report.
29. DEPARTMENT OF THE ENVIRONMENT (1973) *Using Predictive Models for Structure Plans*, H.M.S.O., London, Chap. 8.
30. NEWLING, B. E. (1969) The spatial variation of urban population densities, *Geographical Review*, **59**, 2.
31. DEPARTMENT OF THE ENVIRONMENT (1973) *op. cit.*, Chap. 12.
32. DEPARTMENT OF THE ENVIRONMENT (1972) *New Housing and Road Traffic Noise*, H.M.S.O., London.
33. DEPARTMENT OF THE ENVIRONMENT (1973) *op. cit.*, Chap. 9.
34. *Ibid.*, Chap. 10.
35. BROOKS, J. E. and GREEN, J. A. (1968) *Refuse Disposal in South Hampshire*, Local Government Operational Research Unit, Reading.
36. "It would be more correct to say that participation is an issue of political science and not planning at all." STYLES (1971) *op. cit.*
37. *Department of the Environment Circular 44/71, Memorandum, op. cit.*, paras. 63 and 69.

38. *Ibid.*, para. 72.
39. For development plans, *ibid.*, paras. 61–62, 65–66.
40. STYLES (1971) *op. cit.*; DAMAR, SEAN and HAGUE, CLIFF (1971) Public participation in planning: a review, *Town Planning Review*, **42**, 3.
41. *Department of the Environment Circular 52/72, Town and Country Planning Act 1971, Part II, Development Plan Proposals: Publicity and Public Participation,* H.M.S.O., London.
42. ARNSTEIN, SHERRY R. (1971) A ladder of citizen participation in the USA, *Journal of Town Planning Institute*, **57**, 4.
43. HOINVILLE, GERALD and JOWELL, ROGER (1972) Will the real public please stand up ?, *Official Architecture and Planning*, **35**, 3.
44. Town and Country Planning Act, 1971, s. 8(2) and 12(2).
45. S.I. 1969 No. 1092, *Town and Country Planning (Inquiries Procedure) Rules 1969*, H.M.S.O., London; see also WRAITH, R. E. and LAMB, G. B. (1971) *Public Inquiries as an Instrument of Government*, Allen & Unwin, London.
46. Town and Country Planning (Amendment) Act, 1972, s. 3.
47. DEPARTMENT OF THE ENVIRONMENT (1973) *Structure Plans; The Examination in Public*, H.M.S.O., London.
48. SCHON, DONALD A. (1971) *op. cit.*; WILDAVSKY, A. (1971) *Evaluation as an Organisational Problem*, University Working Paper 13, Centre for Environmental Studies, London.

Index

181